How to Be the Best Lover

A Guide for Teenage Boys

Also by Howard B. Schiffer:

First Love / Remembrances

How To Be A Family
The Operating Manual

How to Be the Best Lover

A Guide for Teenage Boys

Howard B. Schiffer

Heartful Loving Press / Santa Barbara, CA
www.heartfullovingpress.com

The information contained in this book reflects the opinions, experiences and beliefs of the author. By checking with qualified authorities and professionals in this area, every effort has been made to assure that the information contained herein is accurate and complete. At the same time, neither the author or the publisher is engaged in giving professional advice or services to the individual reader. The ideas, information, and suggestions contained in this book are not intended as a substitute for consulting with qualified health care professionals, your family, and religious counselors. Neither the author or publisher shall be liable or responsible for any loss or damage allegedly arising from any information or suggestion in this book.

♥ Heartful Loving Press
PO Box 30041
Santa Barbara, CA 93130

ISBN 0-9723639-0-4
Book designed by Jane Kutcher and Michelle Shapiro, 87 18 Creative Group
Library of Congress PCN: 2003110762
Schiffer, Howard B.
How to be the best lover / A guide for teenage boys / Howard B. Schiffer
Includes index
ISBN 0-9723639-0-4
1. Teenage sexuality   2. Sexual education   I. Title

For Austin

Contents

Acknowledgements

Thank you to Michael Ryan and the Men's Community of Santa Barbara, you who have shown me the best that men can be and helped me to find my place in the circle. To all I have sat with and those who continue to hold the flame; Stevenson, Alex, Barry, Billy, Brad, Brian, Christopher, Craig, Crisman, David, Eric, Gary, Jamey, Jimmy, John L, John D, Larry, Lloyd, Mario, Mark, Reaps, Ronnie, Roy, Sean, Simon, Willie, and any I have forgotten. This book could not have been written without you all.

To Alex Lobba, my brother. I knew you were the first to read this. Thank you for being on this path with me.

Brad Fiedel, composer extraordinaire, whose music can transform and who has played on the big stage, thank you for giving me a thumbs up that there was something here.

Alison Reitz, my first editor and friend, for your immediate enthusiasm and excellent suggestions in getting this book going in the right direction. And always for leading me to Escalante.

Anna Bunting, dear friend and wonderful midwife, thanks for believing in this book and giving your support, information and knowledge.

Jennifer Louden, talented author, you were the one I was most afraid of giving it to initially, because I respect your work so much. Thank you for your tender heart and for believing that this was worthwhile.

Debbie Lowry, friend and educator, for being in the first group of women to give me a big resounding "YES", and for your expertise in this arena.

John Luca, neighbor and friend, whose writing I respect and who gave me important insights and direction early on.

Janice Cook Knight, dear friend and witness to our marriage, thanks for your smile and support. I appreciate your sensitive comments.

Donna Bayet, I appreciate your persistence in getting to review the original manuscript and your thoughtful words and honesty.

Ilene English, counselor and dear friend (how long have we known each other?), for your wisdom and insights.

Sandy Danaher, friend, counselor and wonderful human being. Thank you for your laughter, for confirming the importance of this book, and counseling me through the background process to get here.

Priscilla Stuckey, the best editor on the planet, for your invaluable contribution and sincere belief in this project. I am so thankful to have found you.

Ashley Rogers, actress par excellence and my teenage ambassador. Your validation of this work was critical. Your generosity in getting this out to the teenage community was invaluable. Thank you. We all love you.

Jane Kutcher and Michelle Shapiro, the incredibly talented 8718 Creative Group team who took my words and Ezra Coopers' illustrations, and molded them into a work of art.

Ezra Cooper, Artiste par excellence, who immediately got what this work was about and brought out the heart through his outstanding illustrations. You were so worth the long search it took to find you.

Stevenson Whizin, the best partner in the world and a true friend. Thank you for being you and for being in my life. Your initial confirmation that

I had something was important. You always add value.

And Most of All to Kim, Austin, Zoë and Eliana, you make every day worth living.

Lights on the Horizon

On June 22, 2000, my son turned thirteen. This birthday was not too different from other birthdays, except that he was bored with his annual beach party and opted instead for a party at home. We had thought about a rite of passage, something to honor his transition into manhood, but aside from a conoe trip in the Canadian wilderness, we couldn't come up with anything that felt significant. And, too, in many ways he still seemed so much like a kid.

But I saw lights on the horizon, little twinklings, and I knew I had to pay attention to them. A few months before, at a campout, as we were sitting around with some friends and their teenage daughters, I was surprised when my son declined to go swimming. He stayed glued to his seat as the others ran off to play—unusual behavior for a guy who loves the water. At some point I realized that any movement might have given away the big hard-on sitting in his lap. Around this time also porn sites started mysteriously appearing on my computer. It soon became clear that the time had arrived for one of the things I had put on my agenda when my son turned twelve: the "Sex Talk." I knew that if I didn't cover it, the culture would.

That discussion, originally planned for a one-hour session, soon stretched into a six-month dialogue. During the process I realized I needed to explore and reveal my own discomfort about sex, how awkward it was for me as a teenager, all of the angst and anticipation I experienced, and how I stumbled through my sexual education. It was painful, and it was freeing. (See the appendix.)

Just as we were finishing up and I was breathing a sigh of relief, I realized that the river we had journeyed down was moving quickly into a big ocean, and there was no turning back.

I searched again for books to give my son as a roadmap for exploring his sexuality, but few existed. There were beginner's books, like what we had used in our Sex Talk. And there were advanced books, which were meant for adults and focused on techniques. But there was nothing in between. I wanted a book that would not be shy about the details of sexuality—everything from oral sex to making love—while at the same time being sensitive to the issues involved in opening up with another person on this level.

This book, then, was written as a gift for my son and for other boys who will be discovering their sexuality in the coming years. It is a gentle tap on the shoulder and a whisper in your ear to say, "This is all possible." You can open up your heart, you can find another person to share love with, and you can experience incredible intimacy and ecstasy. And it's worth it.

Howard
Santa Barbara, California

When and Why?

If you are a parent thinking about giving this book to your son, the two biggest questions you need to ask are Why? and When?

Why give this book to your son? The answer is simple: you have an opportunity to deepen your connection with him. Sex is where kids start to separate from their parents anyhow, and instead of abandoning them to figure it out by themselves, you can step in and say, "I'm here to support you and to help you through this transition." You can also be a voice to counter all the awful things this culture says about women and give your son healthier images to hold onto when he enters into relationships with women.

So, when do you do this? Your son is going through the loss of innocence. He's moving from being a kid to becoming a man. But the transition does not take place all at once; it happens over a period of time—and that is what's tricky. Your son may be playing with Legos™, and the next day you're at the swimming pool and notice he has a big old hard-on pushing through his shorts when one of the cute teenage girls comes over.

What you don't want to do is to rush this information just to have the bases covered. The reason is twofold: (1) If your son is not ready for it, he will feel embarrassed and won't know what to do with the information, and (2) He may think you are encouraging sexual activity but may not be ready to take that step, either because he's not yet ready to socialize at this level with girls or his social groups are not yet moving in this direction. In this case, you could be setting him up for inappropriate behavior with a sibling or girl he is friends with or possibly just moving him into a situation that could be awkward and very uncomfortable. For the parent, being in touch with your teenager is paramount so you know when the time is right.

By the time you are thinking about giving your son this book, you definitely should have had your sex talk with him. This is the preliminary "birds and the bees" talk. My talk with my son took months (see the Appendix, "The Sex Talk") and was both very uncomfortable and very rewarding. It was uncomfortable at the simplest level because it takes awhile for a father and son to feel at ease saying "blow job" and "hard-on" and "penis" and "come" with each other. These words marked a line in the sand, and once we'd stepped across it, everything was open for discussion and my son realized I was willing to relate to him on a different level.

Every parent has to decide when and how to cross this boundary, but what is important is the communication. This is not a lecture but an exploration and a learning you are entering into together. Be clear at the outset that you will be going through an unveiling—with regard to your own attitudes about sex and in coming to terms with your own sexual history—as much as will your son.

Having the sex talk gives you an opportunity to open up and establish a relationship so that in the future, when sexual issues do come up, you have some foundation on which to build. If the sex talk has not occurred yet, you'll want to set aside that time first. The sex talk usually occurs when a boy is eleven to thirteen years old, but everyone is different, so trust your knowledge of your son.

The material covered in this book is kind of a "Sex 101." Or, as my son said, "I guess this is the next talk beyond the birds and the bees." If your son is starting to date, go to dances, get physical with girls, has a girlfriend, is making out, holding her closely when they are watching movies—all of those signs and more—it means that he is moving into sexual territory and the time is right for you to give him more information. This book will provide that information. It is the background text, the map of the land, so he has some idea where he is going. He will still need to go there by himself—you (very literally) won't be able to hold his hand— but at least he will know a few landmarks and have some tools to make the journey easier. A child moving into his or her sexuality means a major transition for all of us. This book is a tool to help make this transition easier and, hopefully, a lot more enjoyable.

What You Will and Won't Learn from This Book

This is the book I wish I'd read when I was thirteen. I had this fantasy then that I would somehow find the girl who was the Best Lover in the World. I was convinced that some girl out there deserved this title, and I wanted to (1) find her and (2) make love with her—a lot. I spent hours thinking about who she was and what it would be like.

The reality is that I wanted to know how to make a girl happy (or wild with desire, even better) and to know all the different ways to enjoy each other's bodies. At the time I fumbled along and figured it out piece by piece. Ultimately, this is what you have to do—go through being uncomfortable and awkward and learn with each other about how to be great lovers.

What This Book Can Teach You

But now I know that there is a lot of valuable information that could have made my life a lot easier and less embarrassing and more fun. That's the purpose of this book—to give you, a teenage boy, the information you need on how to be a great lover of girls, of women, and ultimately of life.

This book can be your guide as you learn about being a lover—from your first wet dream to your first experiences with girls. If you're like me, you'll open it and look right away for the chapter called "Doing It" or "Making Love." (It's here as "The Wild Thing" page 104) After all, this is a book on being a great lover, so why mess around? A teacher I liked once said that our culture's view of sex was like the cowboy in a Western who says, "Let's jump in the saddle and ride!" Well, more on that later.

Right now, I want to say that wherever you start, make sure you end up reading the entire book. There's a reason. You'll start to see as you read the book and use it in your life that it all fits together, and this book can show you how.

Now, you might be more concerned with how not to come too quickly or how to make a girl's nipples hard, but if you read the whole book, maybe a couple of times, and then use this information in your life— looking honestly at what does and doesn't work—you will begin to realize that it's all connected. Each step in being a great lover builds on what you've learned before.

Touch is important when you are making love. You may want to pleasure your lover by rubbing her clitoris, but it starts when you are first holding hands. Start to notice your girlfriend's hands. Feel each finger. Go slowly. Then you begin to see how much feeling you can receive and give through your fingertips. If you try to jump into bed to make love with someone before you have the basics down, you will be setting yourself up for embarrassment or an awkward situation at best. There really is a natural rhythm to being a great lover, so follow the information step by step and find out how the pieces all fit together. It is a great puzzle.

What This Book Can't Teach You

Making love, when you are really making love, happens on a lot of levels: physical, emotional, spiritual. When you make love, you get to open your heart to someone other than your family, and in a qualitatively different way than with even your best friend. You have a chance to get way closer to another person than you ever have been before. The wonderful part of this is the physical and emotional intensity that you can experience. The scary part of this is the physical and emotional intensity that you can experience. They are two sides of the same coin.

The physical part of being sexual will drive you to want to experiment with these newfound feelings and sensations, but you may find you're not yet ready to handle the emotions that come with them. Being sexual is complex, and you cannot afford to ignore the new emotional and physical responsibility. If you are shy about dancing with a girl, are you really ready to be completely naked and vulnerable in front of her? You have to decide.

That's one thing this book can't tell you—when you are ready for the great adventure that is becoming a great lover. Only you can check inside yourself to see if you're ready to pay attention to another person's needs as well as to your own and to talk about things that may be uncomfortable or awkward.

Remember that when you are lovers, two people are involved. You not only have to deal with your own body and emotions, you also have to consider another person's body and emotions. However you label them, the issues of responsibility, communication, and vulnerability will be staring straight at you. Are you ready to enter this territory?

Being lovers is a centerpiece of being in love. It is only one component, but it can unleash your fantasies, fears, passion, uncertainty, and desire. Intimacy is the moment when you reveal yourself, for all you are—good and bad—to another person. You have to know when you are ready for this. The timing is your decision.

Letting other people—girlfriends or guy friends—push you will only be accommodating their needs. Don't abandon yourself. Many guys wait until they are in their later teens, and some wait until they are in college. You can wait until you are married or in a very long-term relationship.

So wait until Y O U are ready

I will tell you many of the details and give you all the information you need to be a great lover. But making love is like dancing: you can learn all the steps, but moving easily takes time. And each dance partner is different—in height, in weight, in how big her waist is, in how she responds to your touch and your cues, and in the passion she brings to the dance floor. It is the same thing with every lover—each one is different. And that's the other thing this book can't teach you—what to pay attention to with your partner. If making love is a dance, you want to create it with her, not just lead her in the direction you want to go.

You have to pay attention to what your lover likes. Some girls may want to go real slow and be fairly conservative in what they are willing to try; others may be wild and passionate and really want to experiment with different positions and different places to have sex. But if you're not paying attention, you'll never know. If you come up with one thing that works and then switch girlfriends, you may realize that your old method is totally inappropriate for your new lover. Or if you get into a groove and find something that works and keep doing just that, your lover may get bored and lose interest. It's like singing a duet: the best singers try to balance their voice with the voice of their partner so they can create great harmonies. Working together to create a beautiful song—that's how you have the most fun.

So, read the book. Think about it. Compare it with your own experience. Use what matches your experience and makes sense, and throw away the rest. Or set it aside to reconsider at a later time. I want you to enjoy making love, so here are the pieces of the puzzle as I've come to know them.

And one more thing. A lover, literally, is one who loves. Being a lover is being able to reveal yourself to another person and at the same time to see clearly who she is. Being great in bed always means combining some technical know-how with the openness, honesty, caring, and sensitivity to make a real connection. Learning to love—to slow down enough to recognize the beauty that is in front of you—is your first step on this journey. Enjoy it.

How to Be the Best Lover: The Summary

Who Is the Best Lover?

Qualities to look for in your partner and in yourself.

- Someone who is paying attention to their partner.

- Someone who is willing to reveal themselves—to show who they really are.

- A person who cares.

- A person who can be present in the moment. What is going on right now? What is appropriate? What does my lover want? Is there some thing that needs to be said?

- Someone who is willing to take risks.

- Someone who will communicate what they are feeling.

- A person who takes care of themselves physically, emotionally, and spiritually so they have a lot to share.

- Someone who can laugh and have fun.

- A person who is kind.

- Someone who can find the right balance between going slow and going wild.

- Someone who can enjoy and savor each moment.

Why Do You Want to Be the Best Lover?

- It feels great to satisfy someone you are in love with.

- It gives you many of the tools that are also important to building a great relationship.

- It feels ecstatic to share that type of passion with another person.

- It is a central part of a healthy relationship, and doing it well can enrich the relationship.

- It takes you beyond the day-to-day world and into another realm (of passion, desire, love, caring, and the mystery).

- Being the best lover creates a deep bond between you and the other person. It is a connection that is powerful.

- It changes the nature of your relationship and gives you an incredible experience to share with your lover.

How Do You Become the Best Lover?

- Read this book.

- Pay attention to yourself.

- Pay attention to the person you are with.

- Go slow enough to notice what is going on.

- Enjoy the moment.

- Be in touch with yourself so you know what you need and what you want to do.

- Be willing to laugh and, when appropriate, to laugh at yourself.

- Have interests, passions, things you are excited about that you can bring to the relationship.

- Be in good shape; you can expend a lot of energy with sex.

- Know where your boundaries are, and honor them.

- Know where your partner's boundaries are, and be respectful.

- Be willing to learn—from books, your friends, and your lovers.

- Be honest, and be willing to communicate.

- Take responsibility for yourself and for your partner.

- Choose wisely. Find lovers who have your same values, desires, and interests.

Finding Out Where to learn

about Sex... We say sex is a natural urge,

but we make learning about it difficult and awkward.

Getting information about it is shrouded in secrecy and

shame. If we really believed it was natural and normal, we'd make

information about it easy to get.

But instead, the message from our own embarrassment and the culture is that sex is:

- Very private, in action and word

- Not to be discussed in public

- Something married people get to do but not talk about

- Something to be ashamed about if you get caught being interested in it

- Very uncomfortable to discuss

- A topic that friends can joke about but never seriously discuss

- Dangerous and scary

- Something you'll have to figure out on your own.

Not a very healthy set of attitudes about such an important topic!

So how do kids find out? How can they know?

When I was young I had only a few—pretty bad—sources for information about sex. I had a friend whose dad had access to the porn scene. He always had these eight-by-ten, black-and-white, very graphic photos of women in different poses—a real eye opener for a seven-year-old boy.

We also had porn booklets (I don't even know if these exist anymore) with these little four-by-four pages and poorly drawn pictures—that didn't matter much to us—and very loose story lines about weird people having sex. Nothing romantic, just hardcore in-and-out, smut. Did some dad give these to his son thinking it was sex education? More likely some son stole them from his dad who'd never grown up sexually. We didn't care how we got them, we just passed them around in secret within our group.

"Girlie magazines," as they were known back then—now just known by their titles, Playboy, Penthouse—were only for the visuals. One day I found a stash tucked away in my parents' attic and was told—or I assumed—the workers who built our house had left them there. Yeah, right!

Then there was street talk. The big kid down the street, Freddy Antonucci, told me that the way you screw is to get hard, put it in the girl, move yourself in and out for about three minutes, and come—that's it. Years later I wondered if Freddy had a lot of marital problems.

We also had trial and error. My friend Marco found out that the girl who lived across from him would let him play doctor—and me too—which involved letting us touch her "down there" quickly, when we were about six or seven years old.

I read a lot, too. I scrounged books for these brief, juicy passages. I remember one detective book my dad had that had a couple of romantic sections in it. I must have read those pages dozens of times.

You get the picture. My information was very limited—and distorted at best.

The Porn Superhighway—Going Nowhere

Even today, with the Internet and a much more open view of sex in books, on TV, and in the movies, the information is still limited. Teenagers who are trying to act cool, like they know it all, may want to argue with this. They've seen breasts, they've seen people screw in movies, many have visited porn sites on the Internet. So what else do they need to know? The truth is that much of the information they've seen is at best just surface and at worst pretty twisted.

Knowing what you do in bed—the mechanical part of sex—isn't difficult. I'll explain it in lots more detail later on. But just because it isn't complicated doesn't mean it's unimportant. It's good to know how to give great head, what getting a blow job is all about, the ecstasy of screwing in a shower—those details about what to do and what the possibilities are. All of this helps make you the best lover.

But there's a lot more. If all you're paying attention to is the surface stuff—how hard you are, if she's going to give you a blow job tonight, or how hot her breasts look—you'll never be a great lover. Why not? Because you'll just be paying attention to yourself, for one thing. You'll be missing all the cues your lover is giving you, and you won't get to enjoy the experience of getting really hot and turning each other on together.

And if all the images in your head come from porn sites on the Internet and girlie magazines, then you might have a really hard time making love to a real girl. Don't get me wrong. Porn works. That's why it's such a big industry. But it works for only one thing—getting a hard-on and beating it. If you want to end up with a real girl—and later on a real woman—then having lots of twisted images in your head about a girl getting screwed while giving someone else a blow job might not be the best source of inspiration. It's just not real for most of the girls that you will know, and it will set you up to expect something fake and make it hard for you to connect with the person you are with.

Porn also will set you up to focus on one thing—coming, or, as they say in the porn industry, "the money shot." To go into sex wanting only one thing—the big O—will make you rush through all the steps that get you there. Not the right attitude for a great lover.

Porn makes women and their bodies into objects. Look at enough of it, and you begin seeing them as objects of your desire and not as real people. If someone does this to you—sees you for your money or your status as a musician or an athlete or because you are good-looking—you know how lousy it feels. You're not there. You have become invisible. At first it might feel great to be idolized, but at some point you will realize that the other person is not seeing you; they're only seeing their fantasy. For women it is the same—they want to be seen and loved for who they are. Having lots of porn in your head will only get in the way.

The more you experiment with sex, the more you will figure out how many ways there are to do it. You'll try out different positions for making love, different ways to get your lover hot, ways to have sex in cars or at the beach. But the main way to have great sex is to remember that something is always happening—right now!—between you and the person you are with. If you're just focused on where you want things to go, you might end up missing the real show. Rushing to your hotel room? Maybe you just missed the excitement of tearing each other's clothes open in an elevator. Get it?

Getting Real (Information)

The best way to find out about sex is to get real information you can trust and then run it past your own filter and your own experience. Ask these questions:

- Does this ring true?

- Is this what I am comfortable doing?

- How did this feel when I tried it with my girlfriend?

And then talk.

Talk with people who

1. You can trust,

2. You can trust, and

3. You can trust.

When I Was a Teenager I Was a Sexual Illiterate

As you can imagine, since I couldn't get good information about sex, I didn't know how to talk about it either. When I was in high school, talking about sex with my friends involved only a few questions:

- "Did you do it with her?"

- "How far did you get?" and

- "Will she do it for me?"

Well, we didn't actually ask the last question, more just thought about it, and only when sex was obviously the only reason our friend was with the girl in the first place.

Not very evolved.

I was heavily invested in looking like I knew what I was doing—or at least not letting anyone else know what I didn't know.

Who Can You Talk With About Sex?

Where do you find someone you can trust to talk with about sex? Start with a parent, if you have already established some basis for talking about this. If their eyeballs start to pop out of their heads when you ask them if a blow job is really considered "having sex" (answer: Duh, yes!) you probably are giving them more information than they are ready for. Parents need some time to come to the awareness of their children's sexuality. It's a big transition for them too, letting go of their kids and watching them become adults. Sex is definitely a rite of passage for everyone involved. That's why it is such a big deal.

How about friends? Maybe start with one friend—someone you really trust and who will not go out and blab what you are doing to the whole world. Ideally, someone going through similar experiences so you can share information. Remember, that's the purpose of talking—you are gathering information. So the main criteria is:

Talk with someone you T R U S T
and someone who you can go into some detail with.

With different people you will probably need to alter your details. That is, with a parent you might just say that you just had sex with your girlfriend, since saying "oral sex" might be further than you want to go or more than your parent wants to hear. But with a good friend you might be able to talk about this incredible blow job and how her lips felt on the head of your unit or what her tongue was doing while she had her lips wrapped around your thing.

Who else? Should you talk to your girlfriend? Absolutely—and it's tricky. Absolutely in that if you are having sex or starting to have sex with someone, communication (which we will get into later) is key. This can be as simple as "Yes, I like it when you rub my butt" to "No, I don't like oral sex." At the same time, if you're having questions or problems or confusion, it is sometimes easier to go to someone outside of your relationship to check things out. Why? Because both of you are hooked into what is happening, so it's good to find someone who has an objective point of view.

Again make sure it is someone
you can T R U S T

If the other person is someone who is going to tell your parents or judge you (you dirty sleazebag!) or try to put their own moves on your girlfriend or just voyeuristically get off on your story (their own private porn show) without really caring about you, forget it. This is personal, and you deserve to be treated respectfully and honestly. So:

Choose your C O N F I D A N T S wisely

If you start telling someone and it doesn't feel right, you are allowed to stop. Just say, "You know, this feels off, I need to think about this some more on my own." Don't keep pushing through just because you started. It's your life, and if you don't honor and respect yourself enough to make sure you feel comfortable (and safe) no one else will either.

What Do You Want from the Conversation?

When you are telling someone very personal information, it's important to tell them what you want. You may just want them to listen. Tell them that. Say, "I'm going to tell you about what's going on sexually with my girlfriend. I just want you to listen." If you don't want them to give you any advice, tell them that: "I don't want your opinion or advice." If you do want them to give you feedback, say it. Or you might just want to hear an opinion, not advice, or you may want them to share with you what their experience has been. Remind them that you just want them to be honest.

You should also remind them at the start that what you are telling them is completely C O N F I D E N T I A L and that if they can't keep it to themselves they should tell you now, B E F O R E you start

Be specific. If you want to make sure they won't tell anyone, say, "I don't even want you to tell your girlfriend, okay?"

It's Not Just About You

Remember that there is another person (your girlfriend) involved here. So if you're telling a best friend about the girl you just laid, remember you have to be responsible about and respectful to her feelings too. In the same way that you wouldn't want her going around telling her friends that you were a "bad lay," you want to be aware that she might be embarrassed by being talked about as well. Think about telling your story with her in the room (or at least with her finding out that you told). Would you say, "I gotta tell you, she gave me the worst blow job, she had no clue what she was doing, she was trying to do it without touching it!"? All I'm saying is, be sensitive. Don't tell the story at the other person's expense. This doesn't mean don't talk. It means be aware that this is not just about you. Someone else—a real person who took a chance and got intimate with you—is involved too.

The Rules of Talking About Sex

So how do you talk about "it"?

Rule number 1: Be specific

Whoa, that's a big one. That's where things get a little scary. You get specific, like "Last night I felt so awkward when we said good night. I really wanted to kiss you but I didn't know if it would be ok." and you can just about feel your mouth go dry. Just the fear of being vulnerable and intimate is enough to keep many guys' mouths shut tight. So you might want to take it in stages, one small disclosure at a time.

Going further and actually talking about sex itself is another big leap. Maybe what you have to say is the sex was uncomfortable. Even that is really difficult for most people. But saying that when your girlfriend was giving you head her braces started digging into your member right when you were getting ready to come—that's a whole lot more specific. Sometimes it is easier to just give someone a basic detail, like, "Hey, slow down here, you're going way too fast for me!"

Remember, be information appropriate.
Give the R I G H T information
at the R I G H T time
to the R I G H T person

Every parent might not want to know about how you're conflicted about giving your girlfriend head, and with some friends, you may be talking about something that is too far away from the skateboard or basketball reality they are involved in. Pay attention. Check their reaction. Is the other person drooling? Not good; they're getting off on your story. Are they switching the channel? Definitely not good. You want someone who can deal with what you've got to say without getting lost in their own fantasy, confusion, or boredom.

Remember, you can S T O P at any time

The point here is that when you can be specific, you can start to get real information. European guys are much cooler about this. They seem to be able to get much more explicit, willing to really share details on techniques. If you are starting to have oral sex with your girlfriend and you just went down on her for the first time, wouldn't it be great if you could talk with your friends about how it smelled and tasted and what your tongue was doing and what she was doing with you while you were eating her, instead of just saying, "Oh, yeah, I gave her head, it was great"? You can't start to explore all the possibilities or know where you could go if you don't open the door.

If you are really trying to get information (not just trying to brag to your friends about how much nooky you are getting and what a major stud you are), talking with people about what you are experiencing will help you develop one of the biggest skills in being a great lover; being willing to learn and find out more.

No Virgins in High School

The hard part here, of course, is that in high school no guys are virgins (right?), and every true dude is a studmaster. Okay, in some high school crowds nowadays, guys can actually admit they are virgins, though this is still more the exception than the rule. To admit that you don't know everything or that you want to know more is a major risk. Think about it: How much experience can most guys in high school or at thirteen years old have? Even if they have a girlfriend and are getting laid every weekend, so what? You aren't an expert right away. It is only through having different lovers—or different experiences with the same lover— over a long period of time and having relationships deepen so you can feel safe enough to try out lots of different sexual stuff that you really get experience. Sure, some guys are great lovers when they are teenagers, but really great lovers are always trying to find out more, to learn about love and the person they are with—and you can't do that unless on some level you admit what you don't know (if only to yourself). Most of the guys who are walking around holding their crotch and pushing out their chests and bragging about how many notches they have on their gun are just bluffing.

Feelings Are Telling You Something

So now we come to the next rule for talking about sex:

Rule number 2: Connect it with feelings

Whoa, double scary. My feelings joined the underground when I was about thirteen and didn't surface again until I was in my early twenties. I don't mean they dipped just below the surface, I mean they got buried, deep in the underground, like the catacombs. It wasn't safe for me to have feelings. I grew up in a place where gangs and fighting were the normal everyday thing. I was always looking over my shoulder, wondering who was going to fight or get beat up after school.

Hopefully you still know what feelings are going on inside you. The truth is, you are in a very emotional time. Your body is changing, your social life is going through major shifts, and a lot more is expected of you at school. You may be having any or all of these feelings, maybe even at the same time: passion, excitement, fear, confusion, anxiety, nervousness, anger, love, lust, arousal, pain, boredom, even detachment and feeling unconnected or lonely. It can be overwhelming, and for many young people, the first reaction is to hit the emotional "off" button.

Don't do it. You'll be cutting off one of your biggest avenues for becoming a great lover. (More on this later). Emotional zombies don't turn into passionate lovers. Look around at adults in their thirties and forties who chose to turn off their emotions. They're the walking wounded and still stuck emotionally in their teens. You can choose to go through the feelings, become a lot stronger in your character, mature in being able to deal with the challenges that life throws your way, and have the benefit of being the best lover.

Shutting Down Feelings Is Expensive

All these strong feelings can make it seem pretty attractive to follow certain escape routes, like drugs, drinking, and smoking. Doing these things numbs you out so you don't have to feel so scared or confused—another way of saying it takes the rough edges off the world. It's no coincidence that of all of the people who smoke, 85 percent start when they are about fourteen years old—the perfect time to get hooked on nicotine because feelings are strong and smoking takes the edge off.

Watch when people smoke—before they are going to school or work, before a big test, after sex. What's going on? Those are times when uncomfortable feelings come up—the fear, the awkwardness, the embarrassment—and cigarettes make it a little easier. It's the same with drugs and drinking. Watch the shy person at the party after he's had a beer or two. Suddenly he's feeling fine and ready to get down: "Let's party!"

Drugs work, unfortunately. They shut feelings down—even if that's not the reason people say they are doing them. (Ever heard someone say they smoke because they are uncomfortable? No, they say it looks cool.)

But drugs, alcohol, and cigarettes come with some big price tags. The first price you pay obviously is your health—not a major concern when you're fourteen, but one that is going to get a lot more important as you get older. Also for some kids, their pastime gets to be their main vocation (especially with hard drugs or alcohol), and they don't worry anymore about feeling uncomfortable since they have a new focus in their lives: when can they get loaded or smashed next?

Turning the Feelings Back On Is Difficult

Even if you're not a heavy user, the price you pay for getting into these substances and shoving your feelings into the basement is that you get out of touch. You can't feel. When someone asks, "What's going on?" or "How are you doing?" you really don't know. It's a mystery to you.

So who cares? Isn't it safer not to feel? Not to be vulnerable? Not to have your feelings out there where somebody can trample on them? In a way, yes, but when you totally lose touch with what's going on inside you and you no longer know what you feel about something, you have lost a major tool to make you a great lover. It's true:

Part of making love is E M O T I O N A L ,
and part of being emotional is having F E E L I N G S

Premature Intimacy

For some guys the emotional component of sex really is too much. This is a great reason to wait. Many guys are driven by their sexual urges into "premature intimacy." They run headlong into a sexual relationship, listening only to their unit, and then run out as soon as the conquest is over. They really are not ready for the emotional part of sex, but they don't realize it until after the physical part has been consummated. Running out after the in-and-out is bound to leave hurt feelings in its wake.

For the guys who are ready to deal with the emotional component of sex, the good news is that you can learn when it is safe to connect with your feelings, when to expose yourself, and when to play the tough guy. Walking down the halls at school, you may still be the rock hard "I can take it" guy on the outside. But with your closer friends it may be safe to talk about what you're feeling on the inside, and you'll certainly want to be in touch with pure ecstasy and pleasure (and thankfulness) when your girlfriend is giving you head in the backseat of your car while you are looking out at the sunset.

Admit What You Don't Know

So being able to know what you are feeling (even if it is just knowing that you are clueless) means being able to be honest with yourself. Before you can receive new information, you first have to know (and admit) what you don't know and how you feel about it. And remember, we're not talking here about getting a good mark on a math test, we're talking about giving great head or having incredible sex. The payoff is huge. Sometimes it is worth it to be dumb.

Girls You hear

a lot of talk these days about how

boys and girls are different.

It's kind of like, if you just believe that we're

from different planets, you'll know

why it is so hard to communicate.

The separation starts with blue jumpsuits for boy babies and pink ruffly outfits for girl babies, moves up to truck presents for boys and dolls for girls. Even the marketing for artists (Eminem marketed for guys) and movies (Blue Crush as a "chick flick") is focused along gender lines. Now that you're getting interested in sex, you're going to hear about a lot more about those differences. And one of the first ones you're going to hear is, "Men want sex, women want love."

Is it true?

How would we know? Is there a standardized achievement test for this? (No!) What we do know is that it used to be true. There used to be—and in many places still is—a double standard. A century ago, boys were expected to mess around and enjoy having lots of sex (sow their wild oats) before they got married. But girls were supposed to be virgins until they married, and even after the wedding, they weren't supposed to enjoy "it" (if they did, well, they were likely to jump on any traveling salesman that showed up at the door!).

We all still feel the effects of these old beliefs. Before I was a teenager, girls were supposed to be "pure," and any girl who experimented freely with sex was called a slut or a tramp and got a "reputation" (the modern version of The Scarlet Letter).

And then there's the matter of getting pregnant. (A whole lot more on this to come later.) When it comes to baby making, girls have been held a whole lot more responsible for getting pregnant than their boyfriends have been. It's kind of like the boy couldn't help himself, but the girl should have been smart enough not to go that far.

All this is to say, When it comes to having sex, you may run into some differences between how you and your guy friends look at sex, and how the girls you go out with look at it. You may realize that girls and guys are also judged differently about being sexually active. Maybe, since girls know they'll pay a bigger price for having a baby, they will be a little more cautious about who to go "all the way" with, and when. Or maybe not. National statistics say that teenage girls are having just about as much sex as boys these days. So you may find as much openness to experimenting on the part of your girlfriends as you hear about among the guys.

So when it comes to sex, what do you need to know about girls?

We Each Bring a Gift

We each have something to bring to a sexual relationship and to learn from each other. Guys have powerful sexual urges, and feeling horny is wonderful (although it can drive you crazy sometimes too!). At the same time, if you just go for your own lust and ignore your girlfriend's needs, you will be leaving a big hole in your own sexual being as well. Girls have their own urges and their ways of expressing them, and you need to get clued in by paying attention—to what your girlfriends says as well as how she acts. There is a reason it takes two people to form a sexual union: each of us has something to share.

When it comes to differences, this much we can see: physiologically our bodies are clearly different. Guys in general can reach orgasm (read: come) quicker. This just means that if you start off with having intercourse, without any foreplay (more on this later), and don't try to get your girlfriend excited, you will also probably come before she does and have her waiting and wondering, "What about me?"

Girls' bodies are made so that it is possible to have multiple orgasms, meaning many girls can reach their peak of sexual excitement and release a number of times in fast succession. She may wake up and feel energized after her first orgasm, just now rarin' to go. So what are you going to do after you've had phenomenal sex with her, both exploded and had amazing orgasms, you're physically and emotionally spent and ready to doze off, and she starts playing with your thing, obviously wanting more? Ignore her? Roll over and pretend you're asleep?

Clearly, you're going to find some differences when you start getting close with girls. Even her anxieties may be different from yours—although, if you read between the lines, you might be surprised at the similarities.

He Says / She Says

Here are some things you might hear boys and girls say:

He says: I'm concerned about my acne, or I don't have a lot of hair on my body—am I good-looking enough? Is my unit big enough?

She says: I'm concerned about my breasts—are they big enough? My braces—will they turn him off? Am I attractive enough? Am I fat?

He says: How do I keep from coming too soon? If I can't keep from coming too soon, then what can I do to satisfy her anyway?

She says: What about me having an orgasm? Should I just pretend, or is he going to be concerned about me?

He says: She is driving me crazy. Is she a teaser? I get all hot and bothered, and she walks off.

She says: I love the kissing and hugging. It's fun seeing him get all excited. I'm not sure if I'm ready for sex with him yet.

He says: Will she have sex with me?

She says: Does he love me?

He says: What do I say when she asks, "Do you love me"? I don't know. Can't we just have sex?

She says: Why can't he say he loves me? Does he just want to have sex with me?

When it comes to sex, girls are just as anxious as you are, just maybe not about exactly the same things. And when it comes to differences, there is a magic key: respect. Your girlfriend's feelings are just as important as yours, and if you want to be a great lover, the first big step is to respect her point of view, even when it is different from yours.

Making love early on is often awkward for both of you. It makes sense, it takes awhile to learn how to enjoy this space. If you are both communicating and making sure you are both enjoying yourselves, it can be incredible. Focusing on the differences can just be an excuse to get past the initial awkwardness. If you enter this knowing that there are differences, and that by working together, you can go way past them to find some amazing excitement together, you are on your way.

Working with the Differences, Finding the Similarities

It's easier to understand the differences if you start by understanding one big similarity: both men and women (boys and girls) want to enjoy themselves sexually. They may need to get there in different ways, but they both want to end up being sexually satisfied. When you know what it takes to be a great lover, and you are paying attention to your partner and communicating, you will be able to figure out creative ways for you both to get what you want.

Don't get stuck on thinking it has to be one way. Sex is much more creative than that. Your girlfriend may just love to have you get her off using your hands, while you may find that having sex standing up against the wall is the most exciting for you. You both may enjoy flirting and subtly touching while you're at a restaurant and then build up to some incredible sex later on that night.

Try not to pigeonhole each other. You may not always want to be the macho guy. Your girl might want to be the sexual aggressor (yes, this is true). Assumptions are just that—they may not hook up with reality. You might be missing what is in front of you. You may be getting all embarrassed about getting a hard-on while you are dancing with your girlfriend while she is loving it that she is turning you on. You may be surprised that girls talk about sex just as much as you do. Once you start paying enough attention to see what the differences are, you will also be able to see how alike we are too.

Beat It

Here is another thing that nobody does.

Not you, definitely not your dad, and definitely not movie stars.

Okay, well, maybe once when they were young,

but let's not talk about it.

The truth, though, is just the opposite. Everybody (almost) has done it or is doing it, but no one talks about it.

Knowing How to Enjoy Yourself

Maybe it's the religious dogma or the fear of not being pure, or maybe it's just embarrassing that you can have sex by yourself and really enjoy it. That's a big part of it—to see what you enjoy, to see how you can get yourself off. Because if you don't know how to enjoy yourself, how are you going to enjoy your body with someone else? Not every girl you meet is going to be an expert at giving hand jobs. Some may never have done it but will be curious, and you might have to lead them with your own hand over theirs.

First Shot

Once in my men's group we opened up the subject of "the first shot" or the first time we ejaculated, and it was amazing to see how this was still so embarrassing for many of us to talk about.

These were older guys, who were finally in an environment that was safe enough to begin talking about many of the things we had kept secret for years. The surprise was that we were still carrying around the shame from when we were kids and hiding it—or trying to hide it—from everyone. (One day my dad surprised me in the bathroom—me holding a big hard-on and seriously involved in whacking it. Oops! He just closed the door quickly, and we both pretended nothing had happened.)

IN OTHER WORDS:

Ejaculated, also referred to as came, jizzed, exploded, dropped your load, spilled your seed.

The stories from the various men were great and showed how different it was for everyone. One guy was in the bathroom at his dad's auto shop and noticed some girlie magazines (this was the sixties, and you would still see girlie magazines at auto shops or print shops or sometimes the barber's), and he just started looking and touching his thing with a pencil, slightly rubbing it and going lightly up and down on his shaft, and all of a sudden he exploded—then had to hide the stain on his shirt when he left the bathroom. I remember lying on a bed facedown, with my fist under my penis, moving it back and forth, when suddenly I felt this warm surge come up through my body to my penis, my whole body shook, and it was somewhat transcendental—a complete release.

Everybody Had a Wet Dream

For some guys the first time they come is in a dream (wet dream), and these can happen at lots of different times in your life. Wet dreams are natural, and they show what a strong part your mind plays in getting you off.

The first time it happens you may be dreaming of being involved in some hot passionate romance with some girl you are dying to have sex with, and then suddenly you are inside of her and you explode, and then some part of you wakes up and you realize there is a big wet spot on you or on your bed. Congratulations! You just had a wet dream.

Honoring Your First Time

However it happens for you, give yourself a pat on the back. Many girls these days are getting a lot of attention when they get their first period. Okay, well, they don't wear a sign around their necks at school (Hi, my name is Amy, I'm having my period!), but their moms—and sometimes their dads—consider this a rite of passage and will honor them when they go through it, either with a gift or a special event or some significant occurrence to mark the time.

But no one I know of does this with guys. No one says, "All right, you beat it last night, you exploded—nice going." To be sure, no one does this for girls, either—their first orgasm doesn't get respect like their period does. But at least girls are beginning to get some recognition when their bodies mature and become able to produce offspring—and this is what's happening when you begin to come. It's one of the biggest turning points in your life, and you deserve to be noticed for it or at least to notice it yourself. And maybe that's exactly why no one talks about it—it's way too scary to admit that this is what is going on. You, you little thirteen-year-old kid, can now have a kid. Yikes!

Shaking Hands with Your Thing

The process of beating it is pretty straightforward (with lots of room for variations). Hold your member with your thumb and pointer finger wrapped around it (to form a circle like you are doing the A-OK sign), and start rubbing up and down. You can have a tissue or handkerchief or your underwear or a towel close by to clean up the come after you pop—whatever you feel comfortable with.

A Major Discovery

Here is a tip: Use oil—a major discovery I made after too many skin burns (ouch). Massage oil is great or even a good coconut oil or any hand cream or lotion.

- Don't use anything with peppermint or any deep heat rubs unless you are a masochist—you'll experience major pain.

For whacking it, it doesn't really matter which type of oil you use, but later on, when you get into making love, the type becomes critical.

- Oils and oil-based lubricants (for example coconut oil, vegetable oil, and some massage creams are oil based) break down latex and can make a rubber ineffective. Oil-based lubricants don't break down lambskin condoms, but then lambskin condoms won't protect you from HIV. Some water-based lubricants are available (Astroglide™ is one) that will not break down latex.

Your Greatest Erogenous Zone: Your Mind

You can fantasize in your head to get you excited (this is a great time to play out your love affairs with all the girls you can't have or are just starting to know), or imagine what it would be like with your girlfriend who may just not be ready yet.

My suggestion, as I have said before, is to not go for porn. It lets you have your fantasies, very explicitly, with no complications. But that's just it—they're fantasies at best, and the reality is that they are often skewed. Skewed means off balance, out of whack—focusing on one part of something and forgetting all the rest. It's getting totally turned on by a girl's butt and forgetting there is a lot more to her than that. The problem is that you can start expecting that girls are really like this, or you may need those kinds of pictures to get off, and they're just not real. Besides, there's a lot more in your life to enjoy and fantasize about when you are whacking it.

Not a Public Performance

When you want to beat it, you need to have a place where your dad or sister is not going to come barging through the door just as you are about to explode. In movies when you see someone caught, it's funny. When it happens to you, it's embarrassing.

Also, remember that sound travels. Whether it is your bedsprings going up and down or your elbow slamming against the wall as you are really getting into it, it won't take long for other people in your family to realize what is going on. So if you want your privacy, pay attention to the sounds.

Surprise—Girls Masturbate!

Girls masturbate too. They are also learning to enjoy their own bodies, and that means also learning how to enjoy themselves. They are using their fingers, hands, or a vibrator—a wand with a vibrating motor going inside back and forth—to get themselves off. Further on, when you get into a relationship and you and your girlfriend are away from each other, you can have phone sex, which is just each of you talking each other to orgasm while you are each pleasuring (read: masturbating) yourselves. ("Oh, honey, I'm getting hard just thinking about you"; "I want to put myself inside you—you drive me nuts"; and so on.)

Not Just for You Alone

Also don't think that once you get into a long-term relationship, masturbating will stop. It might, but it might not. There will be times when your girlfriend is just not into it and you decide to enjoy yourself anyway.

Also when you are making love, you both can use these techniques to get each other off, and some people like to get themselves off while their lovers are watching or kissing or fondling them. When you are first starting to make love, and you start coming way too quickly, you may want to schedule a little self-love earlier in the day, which can give you a little more slack. In plain terms, coming at least once earlier in the day means that you won't be quite as likely to explode the minute you enter your girlfriend. Just make sure not to come too close to when you are going to be in bed with your girlfriend, as many guys need a few hours after coming before they are ready to do it again. (This has wide variations, and when you are in a passionate romance with someone, you may be able to make love again and again for hours on end, so know that I am speaking in generalizations.)

Variety Is the Spice

You will also find that there are many ways to get yourself off with your girlfriend as you start to explore each other sexually. You can masturbate by pushing your thing up and down between your girlfriend's breasts or the cheeks of her butt—all very erotic. Again, always use a lubricant, since it makes things move much easier (remember, part of what you are overcoming here is just friction). Keep the oil or lotion close by. You may not want to use it all the time, depending on what you are doing, but often a little extra lubrication makes everything slide much easier.

You might want to try different methods. Guys used to say, "Try a different hand—you'll think it's someone new," as a put-down—as if there was something wrong with you if the only person beating you off was you. But switching hands is a good idea; it will feel different, as will using your whole hand. Trying different places can be fun too. You can just lie in your bed or enjoy it in the shower or lean against a wall.

This is also a great time to experiment with rubbers. Try rolling one on your unit and see how it feels. It's kind of sensuous and can be very arousing. And try masturbating with a rubber on; it's a lot less messy, and you can experience what it's like to come into a rubber. You can also get some practice in taking a rubber off—another important skill because later, with a lover, you'll be using them regularly. Again, what you will start to notice is how you feel when you get off in different ways—great experience for being a great lover.

It's just too bad that so much about sex is still in the closet and that no one talks about masturbating. It is the first sexual experience most people have, and it can start you off on the wrong road if people around you give you the message that it has to be hidden or is shameful. Privacy is good, yes—and you can still be joyous that you're learning a new way to treat yourself with love and respect.

Social Scenes

So now you know. Well, you know a little.

You've gotten some of the basic information down,

you've started whacking off yourself, and you are ready

to get to the next level. But where do you start?

Start Where You Are

You've actually been starting the process all along. In school you've known girls who are friends of yours, who you probably have played with. Maybe you've even had what I will call a "light" girlfriend. I don't mean light in the sense that it didn't mean anything, but light in the sense that you were just as happy playing with your guy friends or doing sports or playing with your bike or skateboard as you were spending time with your girlfriend.

Dance Away

At some point this will change, and your relationships with girls will take on a new level of depth and seriousness. What happens between now and then is that you can try different social situations with girls. Dances are great for this. Just go to a dance, where you can get out on the floor and let your body go and have a great time. It's a great way to start interacting with girls. Maybe you can get to dance slow with a girl, to get close enough to feel her body against yours, to smell her skin or her perfume, to feel her face against yours or her head on your shoulder. You can begin getting comfortable in this new way of being around girls.

That's what social scenes are about: getting familiar with this new kind of relationship to girls. The guys who never have a chance to do this are really missing something. They get a little older, and then they really want to start going out with girls, but they are clueless about where to start.

In some towns there are cotillions—again a dance, but this time one that also teaches you manners. Manners are just the rules for how to interact in a social situation. Like looking someone in the eyes when you are saying good-bye to them. Or asking your date if you can get her something to drink when you are at a party with her. You will get to decide later on which of these rules are real for you and which ones you want to throw away (maybe your girlfriend doesn't want the chair held for her every time she sits down for a meal, although when you go out to a restaurant she enjoys it; or opening the door for her—maybe not all the time but just when you are on a date). You get to decide what works for you, but at least it will give you a place to start and some ground rules for what is expected and what you need to do to fit in.

The Enforcer Says Dance!

It is great if someone at your local dances helps teach people or pushes them into dancing together. At a cotillion in a town I know the instructor is a man who also teaches aikido, so he goes around the dance floor with his big wooden staff—he calls it his enforcer—and pushes people to dance with each other: "You dance with her." There is no room to sit down, and after about three or four dances you forget why you were so afraid. DJs at some parties are sometimes good at this too—they get everyone up to do a line dance, or they lead a game where everyone has to keep cutting in and asking someone else to dance or where the girls have to ask the guys to dance. Or one couple starts dancing and then has to split up and each ask someone new, and then those couples have to split up until everyone is dancing. Anything to get everyone up and moving around is great.

Getting Past Your Fear

For many guys, dancing is very intimidating. You can feel awkward, clumsy, and like you have cement for legs. I took a swing dance class once, and I remember trying to get the basic move down the first night and feeling like a horse who could only clomp on the ground. Embarrassment and fear of ridicule don't help when you are trying to loosen up and have a good time. Often, if you can just get past the initial fear and push yourself out onto the floor, you can end up having a great time.

The Wallflowers

I remember having this experience when I was a kid: everyone sat on the sidelines because we were too embarrassed to join in. Boring! I have seen this happen also at some dances nowadays at middle schools, where everyone is too cool to ask anyone to dance and instead spends the whole dance with their hands in their pockets or standing outside (maybe smoking) or just sitting against a wall—hence the name wallflowers—being lonely and uncomfortable or trying hard to act uninterested. Let the wallflowers stand there holding up the wall while you are out on the dance floor trying to shake down the roof. Who do you think is going to have more fun?

Group Dancing

One of the great things now is that you can do a lot of this stuff in groups. Join a school group, go out with a bunch of friends, or just hang out with some of the guys you know who are at this same place that you are and ready to start trying out some of this new stuff. Even with dancing, you don't have to dance in couples. At some point you'll be in the right situation where this will feel safe and you'll be able to try it out, but for starters just get up with everyone else and start moving. Mosh pits are great for this—just be careful, things can get a little intense out there at times.

Focus on Friendship

Starting out with social situations—if it is with girls you already know, who are your friends—is perfect. What you are really doing here is learning how to be friends with girls. The truth is that for any successful long-term relationship, being friends with girls is essential. It takes you beyond the guy-girl thing and into the heart of the relationship. Being friends with girls has the same qualities as any other friendship:

- You are kind. You extend yourself, thinking about her feelings first.

- You are considerate. You treat her the same way you want to be treated.

- You are honest, even when it is uncomfortable.

- You let the person know she is important to you, in thought and action.

- You show up for her when she needs you.

- You give the relationship your best.

- You make her feel special.

- You check in and see how she is feeling.

- You create time to spend together.

- You stand up for your friend.

- You are willing to confront things when they are off (like "What's wrong? You seem a little unhappy today.").

- You have fun together.

At some point you will hear people say about their lover or partner, "He (or she) is also my best friend." It's one of the highest compliments you can pay to someone—and it's the foundation for a solid relationship.

If you think about it, it makes sense. Even when you are hot and heavy in a new passionate romance, and you are making love for one, two, three hours or even all-night stretches, at some point you'll need to wake up and take care of everyday stuff. You'll need to fix breakfast or talk about something that is upsetting to you or tell what you are excited about or help the person when she isn't feeling well. If you are friends first, and then become lovers, you have a great basis for taking care of the day-to-day stuff and then feeling safe enough to really explore and become sexual partners too.

Get Naked

Remember, when you are lovers, you are literally naked in front of someone else, with nothing to hide, just you and the other person. The degree to which you can stand up and be naked with your lover is a good indicator of how uninhibited and open your sex will be. Hot, passionate sex always involves taking your clothes off—but this isn't the only kind of nakedness. Being naked with your feelings also turns up the heat, and the more open you can be with each other, the hotter your romance. Remember, the woman literally opens her body to let you in, and you give the most sensitive part of your body to her. You can't get any more vulnerable than that. So if there is not trust and safety at the core, you are both going to have a hard time relaxing into your romance.

S A F E T Y and the T R U S T
are at the core of a great sexual relationship.

First Love

When you are first starting out with sex, safety and trust are even more important. If you are a virgin (see "Virgins" page 98) or if you've only made love a little bit, it's awkward the first time. You are nervous about how you are going to perform, if your girlfriend is going to enjoy it, if you will come before she does, if you'll be able to put your rubber on, how to put your rubber on if you're putting it on in front of your girlfriend, or if your girlfriend will have her birth control taken care of.

IN OTHER WORDS:

Rubber, also known as contraceptive, condom, prophylactic, Trojan, scumbag (the nasty name), safety, protection.

And probably most of all, you are wondering if you are really going to get to "do it" this time.

Well, if you are friends first and can be honest about your fear or your anxiety or just be able to laugh together or lie in bed and look at each other and tell stories, you have gone a long way toward being great lovers. Being the best lover is about being able to be comfortable and have your lover be comfortable, and the place this starts is social situations, with learning to relate to each other person-to-person, being good friends.

IN OTHER WORDS:

Birth Control, also known as pill, DMPA (also The Injection, or Depo or Lunelle), the shot, diaphram (not in use much by young girls), IUD (also probably not in much use by younger girls)

Making Out Here is where

things start to get fun.

When you start to make out, you are going from social situations

—maybe with a group or maybe even

with a girlfriend—to starting to get physical.

It's in His Kiss

Some guys will say, "It's just kissing, no biggie." But kissing is a big deal, and if you can't get kissing down and really learn about how to get passionate with your lips and your tongue, you will never be the best lover.

There really is a natural process to becoming the best lover, and if you take every step and really explore it, each one is going to give you the next essential piece of being the best lover. It's like you're taking a long hike, and each step is important to take you to the next place. If you can really enjoy each step as it comes, you will also find out that you are exactly where you need to be to reach the next level.

Time Together, Time Apart

Now you have learned to be social, you have gotten comfortable around girls—or maybe even a special girl—in a more intimate setting than just school or an after-school activity, and you are starting to actually develop a relationship. You're probably doing more things together now—going to the movies, going out to eat, having breakfast together, seeing a play, being over at each other's houses, meeting each other's families, talking on the phone, going to parties, hanging out with friends.

Some things you will do with groups, even if you are a couple, and other things you will do with just each other. Both are important. Both will let you learn about each other in different ways. A healthy relationship will have many facets—time alone with just each other, time together with friends, and time apart.

It is real tempting when you are first falling in love to have the other person be everything to you, but over the long term it is a setup for problems, since people just don't work that way. If you are with someone who only wants to be with you all the time, this may not be a good sign. Mostly when someone wants just you, it is because they are insecure about relating to other people or don't feel secure with you—things they will need to work on by themselves (at some point) to be a whole person.

The truth is that we cannot satisfy all of another person's needs. We need a bigger circle of friends and relationships to fulfill us.

Just the Touch of Your Fingertips

Anyhow, so here you are with someone, and you are spending a lot of time with her, and you are starting to touch each other. Maybe you are holding hands or dancing together, or you might put your arm around her at a movie, or perhaps you walk with your arms around each other's waists. These are all great ways to begin. Maybe you even share a sweet kiss goodnight at the end of a nice date.

Knowing exactly when the time is right for a first kiss or even to hold hands is often something of a guess. Your own nervousness and self-doubt (Does she really like me?) can easily get in the way. At times you may move too soon or with someone who doesn't share the same feelings. That's okay, just back off gracefully.

When the time is right, and you both are obviously into it, enjoy the feeling. Enjoy the rush of excitement at being able to touch each other. This moment is something to treasure. It is thrilling. An old Joni Mitchell song talks about dancing together back in 1957 when they had to "dance a foot apart"[1] (yeah, for real—chaperones used to stand at the sidelines of a dance with their rulers, waiting to make sure there was indeed a foot between the couples). She sings, "With just the touch of our fingertips we'd make the electricity explode."[2] That's it, that's how intense the feelings can be. When you are first starting to cross this threshold, you can get a huge charge from just a first kiss goodnight or getting to hold hands when you are out on a date. I know guys who are a lot older, in their thirties and forties, and sometimes when they begin dating a woman, even now after they've had lots of sexual encounters, they still go slow and really enjoy these first moments.

The Transition Toward Passion

When you are becoming the best lover, a lot of feeling is transmitted in your touch, so here is the first opportunity to be sensitive. Notice how it feels when you touch each other. When you touch your girl's face for the first time, notice how her skin feels, how it makes you feel, how her eyes look at you. All of these are important cues that you will learn to pay attention to when you are becoming lovers. They are all telling you something about that person—if she likes you, if she is nervous or shy, if she is excited too. Watch.

Notice how it feels when your girlfriend touches you. Is it great? Are you a little nervous? Is it driving you crazy with wanting more? The transition from a first kiss or your arms around someone watching a movie or from lying in bed and playing to making out is also a part of the dance. You both have to be ready and in the mood. If you've been doing the groundwork, getting to know the person, spending time with her, sharing parts of what is going on in each of your lives with each other (all the stuff—schoolwork, extracurricular activities, stuff with your families, or excitement about learning a new song on guitar), then the transition will be easy and natural.

It might be when you are lying in bed and have just been tickling each other and you suddenly stop and look at each other and time starts to slow way down. Pay attention to what you are feeling and what your girlfriend is feeling. You will be giving each other messages now, probably not verbally, that the time is right. Be patient. If the time is not right, you really don't want to push this. You can ask yourself some basic questions if you are uncertain:

- Is she giving me messages that she wants to get closer (in how she looks at me, in what she says)?

- Is it comfortable when we are physically close? Is her body stiff and pushing away, or is she relaxed and moving toward me?

- Is she initiating any contact—when we walk together, when we first see each other, when we are watching a movie together?

- Can we play (tickling, wrestling, holding each other) and be physical? Is she comfortable with this?

- How does she respond when we kiss? Does she quickly end it, or does she participate?

- How does this feel to me? Am I ready? Am I doing this because it has started and I don't know how to stop or slow it down? Or am I really into it?

If you have an agenda that you want to be making out with her, it won't work, or it will be awkward. Those movies where the guy forces himself on the girl and she resists and then finally gives in and is passionately making out with him are mostly bull. It doesn't happen like that. It's a mutual decision, and you both have to be ready to open up on this level.

Eating Each Other's Faces

First kisses, even if you have kissed goodnight before, are still on the lips or on the cheeks. Then at a certain point you move into opening your mouth, as your girlfriend opens hers, and you start to kiss with your tongues, touching your tongues, using your tongue to feel her lips and her skin, and having her kiss you back with her lips and her tongue as well.

Lips and tongues can transmit an incredible amount of passion and will be essential tools for your becoming a great lover. When my younger daughter first started seeing people French kiss in movies, she squirmed and said, "Oooh, Dad, they're eating each other's faces." It was weird and scary to her. Obviously this view changes by the time you're a teenager. Get into it. Feel how great it is to be holding someone and have her mouth open on yours, her tongue playing with your tongue, her hands touching your face.

IN OTHER WORDS:

French Kiss, also known as tongue kiss, tonsil hockey.

Great Kissers

Lovers sometimes give each other a great compliment: "You're a great kisser." It says a lot. If you can't get making out down to where you really enjoy kissing the other person, you are going to be a pretty boring lover. The kissing is essential.

And as you get safer with the other person, the kissing and using your tongue will wander all over her body. For now you can start with her face, her ears (having someone put her tongue in your ear and kiss your ear can be very exciting—same with your toes) and maybe a little bit on her belly.

Revealing Yourselves in Time

You are starting to get sexual now, and this is all part of it—opening up your bodies to each other. You first have to start where it is safe and feels comfortable and then move into more intimate places, as it feels right.

You might want to start touching each other with your hands now as you make out. Again, this is consensual—meaning you both have to agree. If you've been making out and your hands are around your girlfriend's waist and you start moving them onto her breasts and she moves them off, get the message. Don't keep trying.

The greatest gift is when someone is ready and she welcomes you—or when you are ready to welcome someone else's touch. To be received is an act of love, and you need to honor it that way. If you are pushing your agenda that you really want to feel her breasts, it will be very difficult for her to find the space to offer them to you.

Also, many people are not entirely comfortable with their bodies, so letting another person in on that level is not easy. It takes a lot of trust. I once had a girlfriend who had one breast that was a lot larger than the other. To me this wasn't a big deal, but to her it was. It took her awhile to welcome me to feel her up, and she never felt that comfortable being naked in front of me. We would be lovers, but she would raise the sheet over her breasts afterward when we were just lying there. Some girls are sensitive about their bellies or their weight. You may be sensitive too—about how much hair you have or don't have on your body, about your weight, about pimples on your face, or whatever.

When you are starting to touch each other, be aware that you need to go slowly. You are revealing yourselves very intimately to each other, and you need to be able to give and receive it as a gift. To explore each other's bodies—feeling each other's hands on your bodies, seeing how kisses or a tongue excite the other person and where—is a great joy. If you really experience this and practice it, you will be taking a major step toward being the best lover.

All great lovers can spend lots of time making out. Even people who have been together for a long time—if they have a great relationship—will find that making out and kissing are still essential. What happens is that you bring whatever is going on with you on that day, at that moment, into your kissing, so it constantly renews itself and is exciting. All you have to do is to be present to really enjoy it.

First Touch The move into

touching each other is big on a lot of levels. Even though

making out will naturally lead into touching,

once touching gets past your clothing and onto skin,

it is a quantum leap in vulnerability.

Bodies on Bodies

Some girls will be passionate about making out, and in these situations sometimes the first touching will be with your entire body. Your clothes will be on, but you will be going through the motions of making love. Her legs may opened up to you, and you will be thrusting yourself into her in your motions, though aside from your lips, no part of your skin will be touching. Sometimes this motion and excitement can carry either or both of you to orgasm, even though your clothes will still be on.

When I was a kid we called this humping or grinding, and it got real hot and very sexy. But your clothes are still on, and sometimes that is the boundary that is needed for some girls to feel safe. They may need to stay at that level for a while (and it may drive you crazy), but you need to understand that even if you are humping into oblivion nightly and kissing with wild abandon, she still may not be ready to have you touch her body. There may be a number of good reasons:

* She may not feel safe enough with you.

* She may not feel comfortable with her body and doesn't want to expose herself to you.

* She may want things to progress more slowly.

* She may feel that this is a boundary that she doesn't want to cross—that it might get her too close to being lovers with you and she isn't ready.

* She may not want to give you a message that she wants a more sexual relationship.

* She may only want to move into touching skin with someone she is

involved with on a long-term basis.

* She may be shy and not want to have this level of closeness.

* She may be concerned about her reputation.

* She may be getting pressure from family or religion or may feel this is wrong for moral reasons.

* She may be afraid of getting pregnant!

You also may be in a situation where your girlfriend is more sexually active. She may be moving in this direction much faster than you are comfortable with. Or you may not feel that this level of closeness is the direction you want to go in with this relationship.

Let the Girl Lead

Touching is something that happens when there is enough safety and trust, and you and your lover are ready to open up on that level. Everyone has different boundaries, but this is a big one for most girls when they are first getting sexual. How do you know when to make the transition? Let the girl lead. She will lead you with taking your hand in hers, starting to take off some of her clothes or yours, or unsnapping or taking off her bra, and you will know that you are ready to take another step in intimacy.

You the Man

Sometimes there may be an expectation that you will lead or be the pro. Besides the danger of moving too fast mentioned above, you may not be ready or may just be inexperienced. In these situations the best thing you can do is to disclose: be honest. Your body is your own, and you have the choice about who to share it with and when. Also, just because you're the man doesn't mean you have to do all the leading or be the expert. Getting to explore this area together can be very exciting.

Breasts Are Sensitive

Oftentimes the first, more intimate, place on her body that you will touch will be her breasts. It may be kissing the top of her breasts, the part that is revealed from the top of her dress or the top of her T-shirt, while you are making out. Again, this level of connection may last awhile; she may not be ready for you to touch her entire breast or be kissing all of her breasts or her nipples. It is subtle, but there are important differences and levels of vulnerability here.

Another clue — B E   G E N T L E .

Girls and women's breasts are sensitive, so you have to determine the level of touch and how your girlfriend likes to be touched (soft touch, massaging her breast gently, just held, playing with her nipple between your fingertips). The same will be true when your mouth and tongue are kissing and caressing her nipple. Be careful—if you're sucking on her breasts, you need to make sure that it is not too hard and that she is enjoying it. You can ask if it feels okay, if it is too hard. If you are paying attention you will probably know. Does it sound like she is enjoying it? It's always good to check it out by asking every now and then—or afterward, "When I was sucking your nipples, was that too hard?" Nipples can also get very hard and erect when a girl is excited. When your hand goes to feel a girl's breast and you get to her nipple and it is hard, most likely it is because she is turned on to you.

Total Touch

There is lots of touching to be done—all over each other's bodies. Don't get hung up on one spot—just her breasts, for example. Her back, her stomach, her arms, her legs and toes can all be very erotic and exciting to touch and lick and kiss. Remember, part of being a good lover is getting into loving or appreciating the entire person. Each person is different. I have found that holding my lover's hips and the top part of her butt can be so sexual when she is moving and we are starting to make love. Some guys love butts and will get totally turned on by feeling them. Again, you have to see how your lover is responding. There are also levels of intimacy that you will reach later on, but for now you are becoming familiar with the intricacies of a woman's body.

Touching You

Your girlfriend at a certain point will also be ready to touch you. Here you also have to determine what you are comfortable with. It may start out with caresses and move to touching and kissing your chest. If she starts moving right to touching your penis, this may be too much for you, and you may need to take her hand away or ask her to slow down. Some girls may think that is what you want, but it may not be appropriate initially for them or for you.

Some guys are very sensitive and erotic with their chests and nipples. Some girls will love caressing and sucking on your nipples too. The same way that you have to be sensitive about your level of touch with them, you need to let them know when something is not working for you. I'm someone who is not really aroused by having my nipples sucked, and in fact it is a little uncomfortable. So I usually either say something or just move my lover's head off my chest if that starts. In the moment it is usually easy to do and still keep the passion going.

Penises Have Feelings Too

Calling someone an "insensitive prick," if you're being literal about it, is really an oxymoron. Our penises are anything but. Having someone hold you too hard can be painful. Rubbing furiously for a hand job can cause a major skin burn and have you limping around bowlegged for a week. You need to let your lover know what feels good. With your words, your sounds, or your hand, let her know if she needs to be more gentle.

Timing Is Everything

Sometimes touching all happens at once, and other times it is over weeks or months that things progress. However it happens, make sure you are both ready and that it is consensual. There are times of intense connection when things will move very quickly, almost spinning beyond your control. You don't want to miss these, for the element of abandon can be very exciting. At other times things build slowly and you get to be amazed as you reach each new level of intimacy.

Sexual Touch

At some point you will be ready to touch each other's genitals.

Maybe you will be making out in your car and she will start massaging your penis on the outside of your pants and continue as your hard-on comes up through the top—or she'll unzip you to get a closer feel. Or you may have watched a movie over at her house, and after everyone else goes to sleep you start making out, and at a certain point, with her hand, she leads you into her panties to feel her vagina. These first touches may be just that, touches only—not an invitation to go any further. You may still be in the making-out phase, only things have gotten a lot more intimate.

Passion Challenge

Keeping the passion from going further can be a challenge at this point, as this level of excitement can build and make it very difficult to go slow or turn the emotions down or off. Your girlfriend may say, "We need to stop." Pay attention. It may not be an appropriate time or place to go any further. Two things you should be aware of here:

IN OTHER WORDS:

Genitals, also known as penis, vagina, dick, cunt, cock, yoni, thing, rod, tool, love thing, twat, family jewels, beaver, stick, pussy, vulva, wood.

- You can never use your strength to force a girl to get what you want. It is illegal, immoral, and just wrong.

- Some girls will "offer" themselves to you because they think that is what they need to do to get you to like them. This is also wrong and something that you should never take advantage of. Sex should be consensual. To be fun, both people need to be there because they want to be, of their own free will.

For guys this can be very difficult. We're often ready to go further and quicker than the girl. Other times you too will know that it isn't right for one reason or another. Maybe you've been involved with someone else that you really need to end things with before you start something new, or maybe you know your best friend is also interested in this girl, or maybe you really know that you would be better off as friends and not lovers. Whatever the reason, listen to your intuition:

- If the time is not right or

- If the place is not right or

- If the situation is not right,

you will be complicating things more by continuing. You need to *stop* and reevaluate what is going on.

New Levels of Responsibility

Be aware that with this level of intimacy comes more responsibility. You are opening up more to each other, and you are both going to be more vulnerable. This will be especially true for first sexual encounters. Things between you aren't as casual as they once were, and you need to be aware of that. When your girlfriend lets you feel her vagina, she is trusting you at a much deeper level. Enjoy it and respect it. This is an amazing time, and I urge you not to rush. Explore with your hands and fingers and eventually your mouth and lips and tongue.

Exploring Her Body

You will first feel her pubic hair (some girls are shaving a lot of it now), but there will often be some.

Feel the outside of her vulva.

Explore the soft folds of her skin—how the skin of her outer lips is connected to her leg and to the even softer skin on the inside of her lips, which will probably be wet with her natural lubricants.

IN OTHER WORDS:

Shaving, also known as a Brazilian.

If she is not wet, pay attention. It could mean she is not ready, or she is nervous, or she is just dry and needs some lubricant or oil. Going down with your hand, you will go over her pubic bone, a soft mound of skin, and then be next to her clitoris, usually the most sexually stimulating spot on a girl or woman.

And then you will find the opening of her vagina, where you will fit when you start doing the wild thing. Behind the opening of her vagina, if you continue with your hand, you will be going to her anus, and past that you will be going up the crack of her butt.

You can look at a picture, but your sense of touch will give you an entirely different picture.

The Center of Arousal

Take your time. It is a very erotic and sexual moment when you get into this level of touch—it is hot and very arousing (major hard-on material). Again, the skin is very sensitive, and there are a lot of nerves here—that's why it is so sexually stimulating—so you need to be gentle. See what your girlfriend likes. She may like a soft, gentle touch. She may want you to start massaging or rubbing her clitoris—the area where most girls or women can reach orgasm. Take note here: it's a myth that her arousal and sexual excitement come from your penis inside her vagina. Even in intercourse, it is stimulating the girl's clitoris with part of your penis, and/or with your hand or fingers, that will get her to climax.

The motion to do this is different for different girls. Some women will like a gentle back-and-forth with the flat part of your finger; others will like it when you take their clitoris in between your two fingers and you are

IN OTHER WORDS:
Vulva, also known as lips, vagina (really the vagina is just one part of it), pussy, beaver, cunt, yoni, twat.

IN OTHER WORDS:
Natural Lubricants, also known as juices or getting wet.

IN OTHER WORDS:
Clitoris, also known as clit, magic spot, love spot.

IN OTHER WORDS:
Anus, also known as asshole, butthole, anal sphincter, back door.

moving them back and forth. Some like you to do light figure eights with your fingers over their clitoris, and some may want you to be rubbing their clitoris gently with one finger while you put another finger inside of them (check with your girlfriend, not all women like this).

Don't Assume What She Likes

Remember lotion, cream, or massage oil if your girlfriend isn't wet. It will make it much easier to create a smooth, exciting, and stimulating motion. Don't assume your girlfriend likes one thing or that she doesn't want you to experiment. You need to be talking to see what is working for her. She may be someone who is conservative sexually, and once she finds one way that excites her, she may be satisfied and not want to get too wild or risqué. She also may just be nervous and uncomfortable about trying new things. This may change over time as she becomes more comfortable with you. Other girls will want to explore this with you and see different things that turn them on. Some girls will have explored this themselves and will want to lead your hand to show you how they want to be touched.

As a great lover, you need to listen and be open to pleasing them. Don't assume that just because your girlfriend is starting to get more and more excited, you have to rub her faster and faster. She may want you to just keep applying steady pressure and keep going at the same speed. At some point you can also start doing this same massaging and stimulating with your lips and mouth and tongue. Some guys don't like doing this, and for others it's a total turn-on. There is no right or wrong, but you need to find out what works for both of you. Some girls can get off only if they are stimulated with your hand, and others can reach orgasm only with oral sex.

Oral Pleasure

Oral sex is similar to what you have started to do with your fingers and your hand when you are trying to pleasure your lover by rubbing her clitoris, but this time it is your lips and mouth and tongue that are doing the massaging. With sex there is often no clear boundary, so when I say that now it is your mouth, lips, and tongue, know that you often will be using your hands at the same time. Your hands might be rubbing her legs while you tongue is feeling around the inside of her vulva.

You may be rubbing her clitoris between your two fingers while your tongue is going a little inside her vagina. You get to be creative here. Remember that in the Indian system of sacred sex, or tantra yoga, there are hundreds of different positions and ways to intensify sexual energy. You are starting to get introduced to some of these, and each subtle variation of how you touch, or what position you are in or your girlfriend is in, will make big differences in your excitement. You have to be a little experimental. I'm leading you into the room, but you need to explore. Remember what I said at the beginning: I'm showing you the basic steps, but you have to dance. Your girlfriend and you have two unique bodies and sets of emotions. This means different things will turn you on, and you will dance (make love) with each other in different ways.

Mr. Happy and You

The other big area of touch, of course, is you and your penis.

It's an old joke: A guy goes to the movies and buys a big container of popcorn and cuts a hole in the bottom and then puts his hard-on through it so when his girlfriend reaches for the popcorn she will be touching him. Take it from me: this is only a male fantasy or a crude joke at best. If your girlfriend isn't ready to touch you, why would you want to trick her into grabbing your thing? Do you think the feel of it would be magic and she would instantly start moaning? She would probably scream, and there would be popcorn flying all over the movie theater!

Room for Her Timing

Girls can be as sexual and aggressive and intense as guys, but each person is different and their sexuality will manifest in a different way. Guys can usually be sexual and aggressive pretty early on, whereas many girls get really hot only after you've made a romantic connection and they feel really safe with you. If you are always the aggressor and always moving your girlfriend toward an end (making love, giving you a hand job, or whatever), you will not be leaving enough space for her own sense of timing and her own sexuality to take charge and start initiating your romantic exchange. You need to leave some room, and for guys with testosterone (the male sexual hormone) surging through their blood at a Mach 2 speed, this isn't always easy. You are going into a beautiful bedroom, and there is an incredible jewel hidden in there, but if you don't slow down you may never find it.

Touching You

Trust me, there will be a time when your girlfriend is ready and excited and interested in feeling and playing with your penis. You may want to lead her down there with your own hand over hers (with her consent, without force) to show her how you want to be rubbed or stroked. Remember, she may be as insecure as you are about this, so be sensitive. All guys will be different. Some guys will just want the head of their member rubbed gently in a circular motion with the palm of a girl's hand. Others will want the shaft of their penis stroked up and down. You may want your testicles played with or gently massaged.

You have to communicate, either with your hand or voice or sounds (sighs, moans) to let your girlfriend know what is working for you. You also have to let her know if she is holding you too hard or rubbing too fast. You may just want her to hold the head of your penis for a while. You have to listen to your body and find what is erotic for you. It may change from day to day. Also, you may have boundaries where some things do not feel safe, the same as she does. Maybe your nuts are too sensitive and you don't want her going there. If so, tell her.

IN OTHER WORDS:

Testicles, also known as balls, family jewels, gonads, nads, scrotum, nuts.

Remember to use lubricant too. You can put some on, or you can have her put some on. It will make things go much easier and be much more enjoyable to you. A little massage cream or hand lotion, or even a vegetable oil like coconut oil, will go a long way toward increasing your pleasure.

- *Warning:* Make sure, if there is any chance that you are going to end up having intercourse, that the lubricant is water based, like Astroglide™. Oil-based lubricants, like hand lotions or vegetable or coconut oils, can break down the latex on a condom and make them ineffective. Lubricants can also cause a condom to slip off if it is applied before the rubber goes on, so just be aware.

We're talking about reducing friction here, and cream or oil will make things easier and more sensual. The speed, of course, is what you have to figure out together. Some guys like to be driven wild by the girl bringing them to excitement slowly. Some guys want it fast and furious—"Don't stop!"

Know that when your girlfriend starts playing with your thing the first time, she may not have it in mind to bring you to orgasm.

This may drive you a little crazy, so try using this energy for more erotic kissing and hugging. At the point when she is ready or it happens, enjoy it. You and she will also find what you need to bring you to orgasm. It may be rubbing up and down on the shaft of your penis while she is holding your family jewels (gently). It may be her just working your head and occasionally going down over the entire shaft. Let her know what is working for you.

IN OTHER WORDS:

Orgasm, also known as ejaculation, come, whiz, jizz, jam, explode, pop, ejaculate, cream.

Oral Love

The next big jump after just using her hand (read: hand job)—and don't get me wrong, you can be real creative here; if she is open to it, you may find that the inside of her elbow is great or between her breasts; it's all possible and open to exploration—is her mouth, affectionately known as a blow job.

Public Service Announcement: Basic Hygiene

Now we have to cut off here for one second for a brief public service announcement regarding personal hygiene. Before you are going to offer yourself (you kind guy, you) and let a girl give you a blow job, it is proper etiquette to make sure you are clean. In the heat of the moment this will not be your first thought: "Oh, excuse me, I have to go to the lavatory and wash my unit." No, you will be thinking, "Hallelujah, my day has come. Yippee!"

Here is the problem: when you start getting sexual, you and your girlfriend can start passing candida or BV (bacterial vaginosis) back and forth, especially if you are uncircumcised. These bacteria are uncomfortable, itchy, can affect a girl's immune system, and are a pain to get rid of. So your level of responsibility here is that if you are going to be getting a blow job, or think you may, make sure you have washed or showered in the last twelve hours and are clean. It's not that complicated, and if you don't want to appear like some clueless geek after your girlfriend gets a yeast infection and wonders how it happened—"Gee, I don't know"— then pay a little attention to personal cleanliness.

IN OTHER WORDS:

Blow Job, also known as sucking you off, giving head, oral sex, playing the mouth organ, fellatio.

STIs and HIV

Another big thing to consider here, once you get close to exchanging bodily fluids (I know that sounds technical, but that is how it is referred to by public health people, and that is what come is, a fluid from your body): you now have to take a big jump in responsibility and consider STIs (sexually transmitted infections) and HIV.

Note: STIs (sexually transmitted infections) are the new term for STDs (sexually transmitted diseases). I think some of the public health people felt like a "disease" might be too much of a stigma and discourage people from seeking help.

STIs can cause sterility in men and women. That means it can make it impossible for you or your girlfriend to have children. Yes, it's that serious. Yuk. Just when you were getting close to having a lot more fun. Everyone knows, though (or should know), that genital warts and chlamydia (the two most common) are a major problem, in addition to herpes, syphilis, gonorrhea, and HIV/AIDS. Also HPV (human papilloma virus), of which there are more than sixty types, in some cases can cause genital warts, and some types are associated with cancer of the cervix, vulva, and penis, and most have no symptoms. Condoms offer some protection from HPV, but the virus can "shed" beyond the area the condom protects. Also hepatitis-B virus is spread in saliva, semen, and blood by kissing, oral sex, and intercourse (condoms offer some protection). Some of these infections or diseases are curable or treatable, but all are a major pain, some are a lifetime commitment, and most can cause death if not treated.

IN OTHER WORDS: *Come,* also known as cum, jizz, semen, sperm, juice.

Sex and Death—No Fun

When you are young it is hard to imagine your own death. That is part of being young—feeling invincible. The danger is that by the time you have made these decisions (or not made them, and something "just happened" because you weren't careful), you could end up living with something your whole life that could have been prevented easily. Making a decision like this only for yourself is one thing (not advised but at least you are affecting only your own body), but when a partner is involved, you are affecting her life as well. So there are two rules here:

Be C A R E F U L.

You have to communicate and disclose.

This means T E L L   T H E   T R U T H about anything you know that could affect your lover's health or well-being.

Again, the difficulty here is that when you are getting close to sex, even oral sex, the last thing you want to do is to disclose that someone else gave you a blow job last week and you know the other girl has a reputation for being with a lot of guys. But you have to—it just is the right thing to do. You also want the same consideration from your girlfriend.

Disease Travels

Nowadays, unless you are both virgins, you have to know that girls can be just as sexually active as guys. This means that your girlfriend may have had sex with someone else before you (it is true—shocking I know), and even if they weren't infected with something, it could be that their partner was with someone else who was with someone else who . . . You get it; disease travels. That is how epidemics have been spread. And the sexually transmitted diseases that have been rampant in our culture in the last while have been spread because many people nowadays have had multiple lovers.

So you have to be careful. Using a rubber, even for a blow job, will protect your girlfriend in case you are infected. Don't plan on taking your thing out of her mouth at the last second before you come. It may not happen like that.

Also, disease can be spread in the form of the fluid that comes out before you actually ejaculate. Also, if either of you has genital herpes (a virus that can stay in and around your genitals, similar to a cold sore that you get on your mouth but possibly more uncomfortable), you probably need to discuss it and abstain (no oral sex either!) until the eruption goes away. If you don't, you will be passing the virus back and forth, since even condoms don't offer protection because the eruption may be outside of the protected area. Genital herpes is also one of those viruses that can last a lifetime—no fun.

Sexual Courtesy

It sounds stupid, but it really is a courtesy: if someone is going to give you oral sex, don't give them a disease. It's not polite or good manners.

No Red-Letter HIV

On a final note, it is really hard to know nowadays who is infected with HIV and who isn't. Tests don't always show the problem, and it may take awhile (sometimes years) for the disease to manifest. Also, someone does not have to be gay or even promiscuous to have gotten a disease. Much of the AIDS in some parts of the world is passed along by straight (read: heterosexual) people, men and women. You can get HIV from blood transfusions too. This means that even with good intentions, you and your lover may not know.

Safe sex means not taking any risks. That is what people who are in the sex business (read: prostitutes, whores, hookers) do. They require their customers (read: johns, tricks) to wear a condom. They can't afford to take a chance.

Back to Oral Love

Now back to our story. For those of you who are getting close to this level of intimacy, it may seem like the biggest bummer to you: Why do I have to deal with this? Without sermonizing, it is just because you want to be able to live a healthy life.

Okay, so now your girlfriend is ready to perform fellatio, she wants you in her mouth. Yippee! Giving head is a very literal description. Her head is between your legs, and your thing is in her mouth. This is a new level of intimacy. Again, she may want to start slowly. Remember that she may not be comfortable doing exactly what you want her to do; she may need to go at her own pace. Girls can also be anxious about their sexual abilities, and she may be nervous about not doing something right.

When she is ready, she may want to start with her lips and tongue over your entire penis. She may want to start licking your member and putting it in her mouth occasionally. You may want her to be massaging your nuts or rubbing your butt at the same time. You have to see what feels good and let her know. It's that old communication thing again. It doesn't have to be a formal announcement: "Honey, can you take my entire unit into your mouth right now and start sucking it while I push it in and out of your mouth?" It may just mean telling her with your sighs that this is incredible or using your body to move or thrust a little when you are in her mouth.

Also remember, you are vulnerable here. Teeth around the head of your penis can hurt or be uncomfortable. And braces—be careful of them, they can be painful too. You need to let her know what she needs to do to be gentle.

Size matters here. If you are too big or her mouth is too small, she may not be able to take you into her mouth all the way. You have to be sensitive to how much of you she is comfortable having inside her mouth.

Relax into Orgasm

A blow job can bring you to orgasm in lots of ways. It may be with you inside her mouth, it may be a combination where sometimes you are in her mouth, sometimes she is working your shaft with her tongue and lips, and also using her hands to stimulate your butt or your family jewels—it is all erotic. When you do come, try to relax your legs and your body and let the energy flow through you. It can be very intense and an incredible release. If you are practicing safe sex, you will come into the rubber you are wearing. If not, you can just come onto your own body or hers or the bed you are in or the blanket you are on.

Afterward

Just relax afterward. Enjoy the moment. Feel the stillness around you. Some guys may be ready to fall asleep now. Just be aware that there are two of you in bed. If you have just come and your girlfriend hasn't, you may want to check in with her (either verbally or by initiating some touching) and see if she wants to reach orgasm too. (Likewise, after you have just given her head and she has had an orgasm, she may be ready to stop and you may need to let her know that you need some stimulation too.)

At some point you may want to clean up your come with a washcloth (before too long) if you plan on sleeping in this bed and don't want to have the wet spot disrupting your sleep or noticed by someone's parents. If you are wasted and just too tired to deal with a wet spot, just put a towel or a T-shirt over it and go to sleep.

If you and your girlfriend are absolutely positive you have no chance of STIs (only if you are both definitely virgins and have had no sexual experiences with anyone else), she may like to have you come in her mouth but may not want to swallow it. Or she may enjoy swallowing it. (When I was a teenager the rumor was that it was high in protein; I don't know if this is true, and I've never seen it recommended on anyone's high-protein/low-carb diet plan.) Again, the tremendous risks here are dangerous (read: life threatening) diseases, so you have to be really careful.

The disclaimer here is that until you are into a long-term committed relationship and have both had negative tests for STIs and AIDS, safe sex will always be the most responsible and sanest way to go. You can have very hot and passionate sex and still be safe; you just have to know where the boundaries are.

Danger Zone

Boundaries are a way to

keep things safe and make it work. When sexual feeling is

running hot and heavy, it is easy to rationalize things

(some people might say anything)

or do things that are not appropriate.

The perspective I am going to share is what works in the long run.

You Are Responsible

The first danger zone and the most basic bottom line is: Don't ever have sex or sexual encounters with someone a few years younger than you (for example, if you are eighteen and the girl is fourteen or younger). This is especially true with girls who are thirteen years old or younger.

You Be the "Adult"

Sometimes younger kids can be very sensual and sometimes a little bit sexual, so you have to draw the line about what is comfortable and where you should stop. For example; tickling is fine (if it is okay with them), but touching their genitals (even if it is okay with them) is not. You have the responsibility to stop something that is going toward being sexual. That is why it is against the law and why you have to be the one to stop it: when you are older, you are the "adult" or the more mature person, and you have to take responsibility. Some kids will do anything to get attention, and they don't have the maturity to know they can be taken advantage of to satisfy someone else's sexual urges and pleasure. Here's the rule:

The older person is A L W A Y S the one who should be drawing the line with inappropriate sexual conduct with a younger child.

No Betrayal

A younger sister or relative is also someone you might think about focusing sexual energy on when you are first becoming familiar with it. This is another danger zone. It can happen because your sexual feelings are up and your siblings or cousins are close by, but it is an important boundary never to cross. With a younger sister or cousin, the reason is simple: for most of their lives girls are going to have to deal with sexual energy from a lot of guys—classmates, guys on the street, friends, men in stores—a million times a day. There should be some relationships that are free from that type of sexual come-on, that are safe—and yours should be one of them. Their relationship with their dads should also be safe— something they can trust. That is why it is so traumatic for girls who are abused by their siblings or dads—it is a betrayal on the most basic level. It also really confuses the relationship and makes it hard (and sometimes impossible) to put back together. The hurt can take years and years to heal. I know women who are in their thirties and forties who are still carrying around the hurt and pain of being violated (read: fondled, raped, or sexually abused) by a sibling or parent. It is a big deal, so keep a very clear boundary with sisters and cousins.

Gossip Says More About You

Another big danger zone is not respecting your lover and gossiping about your experience with her. This is not about trying to get real information from a trusted friend or parent about something that is going on in your sex life. In those situations, you don't even have to name the person, although if it is someone you've been going out with, it will probably be obvious. What I'm talking about is bragging just to bolster your ego—"I'm a major guy, I banged her, whoa, look at me!" Not cool. Sexual bragging says more about you than the person you are talking about. It says you use people and don't really care about their feelings. Think of how you would feel if she was right there—you'd feel like a worm, and if you didn't, you should. If a girl is getting intimate with you,

89

you need to show some respect for the fact that it happened, which means not blabbing it around to your buddies and making it cheap.

If you start talking trash about someone you were just lovers with, it will make you trashy too. Remember, you were there. Don't degrade someone for not being a "good lay"; if you were in bed with her, why didn't you do something to help make the situation better? Think about if some girl were laughing at you and labeling you a "bum lay" (read: very poor performer in bed) and hadn't said anything to you at the time, how would you feel? This falls into the category of cheap talk that doesn't really serve anyone. Stay away from it. Remember what Aretha said: "R-E-S-P-E-C-T."[3] By respecting your lover, you are respecting yourself.

Treating someone with kindness and respect, especially someone who has had sex with you, is kind of a bottom line. Even if the relationship is not going anywhere or is over, when you treat that person with kindness and respect, she will always appreciate it, and it will show that you are a class act. It will also show the next person you are with that you don't just throw people out or trash them after a relationship but that you treat people well and honor the fact that you once shared something with them.

Wait for Consent

There is always a danger zone regarding consent. If someone doesn't want you to feel her breast or give you a hand job or let you put a finger inside her vagina or make love with you, you've got to accept that. You can try to get clear on why:

- Is it too soon?

- Is she not attracted to you?

- Does she want to just be friends?

- Are things going too fast?

- Does she want to save that type of intimacy for when she is older or in a more committed relationship?

- Maybe she just isn't sure.

- Maybe it just doesn't feel right or good to her.

- Maybe she's too embarrassed or conflicted and can't talk about it.

Whatever the reason is, you need to accept it and deal with it. Women are not turned on by guys who don't listen to them. If she says no, don't keep pushing, trying to find a way to get her into bed. If she's not enthusiastic, how great will the sex be?

Magic Potions

When we were kids, you could find these ads in the paper for "Spanish Fly," which was supposed to drive a girl crazy with desire. We were looking for the "magic pill" or trick that would make girls desire us. I once knew a chef at a hotel who told me that if you wanted to get a girl hot, you just put a carrot lengthwise under the backseat of your motorcycle and take her for a ride down a bumpy country road. Now I know she would probably just get sore or chafed and wonder what the hell was wrong with your motorcycle seat.

Magic potions have been around for centuries. Aphrodisiacs are just herbal potions that supposedly awaken the erotic juices.

Today there are even more drugs around, like GBH or Rohypnol, the "date rape" drug.

This is a dangerous drug that makes you have temporary lapses in memory, so supposedly you can mix the drug up in a girl's drink when she is not looking, have sex with her, and not have her remember it. No one tells you that she can also become paralyzed from it and even end up comatose, not to mention that it is illegal and you can be in jail with a rape conviction.

IN OTHER WORDS:
Rohypnol, also called ruffies, roche, R-2, rib, rope, roofies.

Of course there is always just plain alcohol. Getting really smashed may be what some guys think they need to get their girlfriends in bed. If someone needs to be blotto before they want to sleep with you, how big of a vote is that for a passionate connection? In general, drunks have a lousy reputation for being great lovers. It makes sense—they're only half there.

Honor Her Will

The idea behind the drugs or the alcohol is always that if you can use some magic potions, you can turn your girl on, almost beyond her will. That is the danger and the boundary that should never be crossed.

You should N E V E R push someone beyond her will.

If someone doesn't want to do something, why would you want to make her? The reason, of course, is that you are trying to satisfy your own sexual desires, but you are using someone else and not thinking or caring about her feelings. Not okay.

Remember, sex is about trust and safety. Great sex is always founded on those two pillars. If you are trying to manipulate someone into bed, you have a lousy basis for both. Even if it works, where are you going to go from there? There is no future.

Respect Yourself

You are also not respecting yourself or trusting that the right girl at the right time will want to get sexual with you. To think that you have to trick someone or drug her or get her drunk to want to be with you is a sad state of affairs. It means she really doesn't want to, so deal with it, accept it, and wait for things to develop (or not) or move on. John Lennon said once that it was a real sad thing for guys when they had to hire hookers to have sex. He meant that they couldn't find a girl to get sexual with so they had to pay someone to do it. It's kind of like that— you want to find a girl who will be with you of her own conscious will, when she is in her right mind and is doing it because she cares for you and about you.

Making Love with No One There

You'll also learn pretty fast that being with someone when she is sloppy drunk or stoned is not a turn-on. In fact, it's a turn-off. The other person is not really present most of the time; she's into her own fantasy more than into connecting with you. Remember that sex is all about connecting with someone else. If one of you isn't present, it will not be possible to make that connection.

Loving Friends

The other danger zone, or possibly danger-maybe, or at least danger–be aware, is friends. It is real common and easy to transition from being friends with a girl to wanting to have a sexual encounter with her.

Sometimes this can be great. You have a lot of history with this person, it's fun and safe already, and a sexual encounter can be very enjoyable for both of you. The "be aware" part is that sex is not that easy and uncomplicated. Feelings get involved, and things change. Guys sometimes have a hard time transitioning after sex is involved. Either they end the relationship immediately, or they want the sexual element to be the entire focus, or they want to be boyfriend-girlfriend. It isn't easy making or handling this change. Even if it was a one-night fling, your relationship will have a new dimension. You may not want to have to deal with this every time you see her. It may make it more difficult to stay friends or to go back to being friends. Don't treat this too casually.

Lots of times friends get romantically involved for a period of time and then sometimes go back to being friends, but those transitions take lots of work. It is worth it, in a big way, to keep your friends—they can stand with you through many of the trials and passages in your life—but you have to honor those relationships and take into account that what you do will affect them. So think and talk about this before you move forward.

The Strong, Silent Type

Noncommunication is a danger zone too. You can't retreat or become the silent man if something isn't going your way in a sexual relationship. Well, you can, but it really is not fair. You have to let your lover know.

If something is wrong or just doesn't feel good, you have to say it out loud. You also have to demand the same from her.

You can't keep your mouth shut and not speak the truth just because the sex is hot (like your girlfriend is saying "I love you" and you know you either don't love her or are not even sure what "loving" someone really means). *You have to say as much as you know at that moment.* Even if it is that you are confused and don't know.

Don't start T R A D I N G   O F F honesty
for sex because the sex is great.
It will come back to get you in the end.

If something doesn't feel right, you have to check it out. You have to honor your own feeling and ask, "What is going on here?"

You also can't check out of one relationship and drop into another one without letting the first person know what is going on. This just isn't a classy thing to do, and it is a bottom line for how you want to be treated too. Before your new relationship begins going anywhere, you should say, "Hey, I have to clear this one thing up with my old girlfriend before I start this." At some point you may have someone fall madly for you and just dump the other person she is with. Pay attention to that. If she dumped that other person for you, someday she may end up dumping you when the next new guy comes along. At the time you won't believe this and you will talk yourself into thinking that the old guy was just a jerk, but watch out.

Everything Is Revealed Early On

Often everything you need to know about a person is revealed early on in your relationship. The problem is that most of the time we aren't paying attention or, probably more accurately, don't want to pay attention. We try to talk ourselves into just looking at the good parts. But the other parts are there, and if you don't start communicating about them, they could hurt you in the future.

It's the same on your side. If you have some issues that someone should know about (like "I'm really afraid of getting sexual because I don't have a lot of experience" or maybe "I was hurt in my last relationship and I am afraid of getting hurt again"), you need to let the other person know—not on the first date, but at an appropriate time when you are building more trust and things are moving in that direction.

You also get better the more you talk about things, and you will feel a lot of freedom when you start to reveal some of your secrets.

It's a lot of work
keeping things H I D D E N .

Again, always remember that you have to choose when and who to tell.

Levels of Trust

With different people you will have different levels of trust, and you need to be sensitive to this. You don't want to dump a whole bunch of intimate details about yourself on a first date. It's too much. This is what happened when personal ads first got popular— people revealed way too much about themselves on the first phone call or at the first meeting, and things couldn't evolve at a normal pace. On one level it was good because you didn't waste time with people you weren't aligned with on important issues (like sex, having kids, being monogamous), but my experience is that it also didn't allow any magic to take place. And most important, people were giving away too much of themselves before really checking out the other person to see if they could be trusted.

I think this also happens on the Internet sometimes. People get to this false level of intimacy really fast. They tell people the real personal stuff about their lives because it seems like the atmosphere is safe. After all, you've never had to deal with the other person face-to-face! People then get confused when they meet in person and find out things are not quite so easy. Our minds—our ability to put our thoughts down into the computer—are only one part of ourselves. Our bodies, our emotions, our way we take responsibility in the world, and so much more make up the whole picture.

Meeting someone and letting things evolve at their own pace really works. It takes awhile to really know someone, and if you take the time and pay attention, you will find the right time to reveal yourself. With some people, even some friends, it may not feel safe enough for a long time, or even ever, to get to your more personal stuff. You have to trust your intuition while not letting your fears stop you from taking the risk at the right time with the right person. It is not a contradiction, just a delicate balance.

What you will find is that heart-to-heart communication is central to being the best lover, and it's a real gift. So it is always worth it to begin working in that direction. The first time you open up (and every time thereafter), you are taking a major step down the road to being a great lover.

Virgins

Virgins have not always had a great time of it. Remember, they were always the ones getting sacrificed on the altar or thrown into the deep pit to appease the gods. Maybe that is still why no one wants to admit to being a virgin —it could be hazardous to your health!

Obsession with Virgins

With the double standard that was around for so many years, boys always wanted their girlfriends to be virgins. Knowing you are the first one to make love to a girl, and that you are getting to lead her into the mysteries of being a lover for the first time, is really exciting. It also helps minimize the whole jealousy factor since you know you're the first to reach this level of intimacy. But by the same token, being a virgin, for a boy, meant having to admit that you still had not gotten laid and were very inexperienced. I think this is still a stigma for guys especially. It definitely was when I was a teenager. Every year past thirteen that I went without making love got more and more stressful—especially because I was hanging around with older guys who were making what were called their first "conquests." (Sounds like Atila the Hun—not so romantic.)

Boys and girls both can feel a lot of anxiety about the first time.

Girls are wondering:

- Will it hurt?

- Will I know what to do?

- Will I bleed? (see section on "First Time Awareness" in "The Wild Thing", page 116)

- Is he going to like my body?

- And of course, Will I get pregnant?

Boys are wondering:

- Is she actually going to "do it" with me?

- Will I be good in bed?

- Will I be able to satisfy her?

- Will I be big enough?

- Will I be hard? Will I be able to stay hard?

- What if I look like I don't know what I'm doing?

- Is she going to like my body?

For both boys and girls, the stress of the first time can lead to a lot of confusion, concern, and sometimes bad decisions.

Bad First-Time Decisions

I remember once in college a girl asked me to be lovers with her. This was someone I knew only casually, and the reason she asked me was that she was a virgin and wanted to be lovers with her boyfriend but didn't want to let him know she was a virgin. Becoming lovers with someone for a reason like this doesn't make any sense. She would have been much better off making love with her boyfriend the first time, but the stigma of being a virgin and being in college was too much for her to handle.

I have heard this story from many other guys and girls—about the first time weighing so heavily on them that they ended up making love with someone who had a reputation for being willing to "do it" with anyone. I know a girl who met some guy in a bar and lost her virginity on a one-night fling just to "get it over with."

Here is one truth that may make it easier:

E V E R Y O N E is a virgin
at one point.

Obvious, but important to remember. The other truth I have found is:

The R E W A R D comes not from losing your
virginity at an early age but rather from
making L O V E the first time
with someone you C A R E about.

Making Love Takes Practice

Making love for the first time can be somewhat awkward. It's just like anything else—it takes practice and being familiar with what is going on to get comfortable with it.

I know of young people who waited until they were with someone they cared about but still had uncomfortable first experiences. Sometimes the boy and girl are both virgins, neither knowing exactly what to do. The boy might come immediately, sometimes before he even enters the girl, and then be embarrassed. The girl might get really scared and not be able to relax and have a good time.

IN OTHER WORDS:

Coitus, also known as intercourse, lovemaking, penetration.

That is part of what this book is about—to give you enough information so you can proceed at a pace that works for you and hopefully have an enjoyable first experience of coitus.

Nothing to Hide

As I mentioned before, there is something about just being naked in front of each other that can be embarrassing. If one of you is a virgin and has not had other lovers, it just takes a little getting used to. Nothing much is concealed. You may not feel great about your body—most people don't. You are too gangly or too small or have no hair on your legs or have big ears or your penis is too small—it's always something. For girls this is true too, so you again have to be sensitive. You may see a gorgeous girl before you while she may be uncomfortable because her belly is too big or her breasts are too small. Here is where noticing how she feels and letting her know "You look beautiful" can go a long way.

Everyone wants to be the best lover, and since you are a virgin it means that you have no experience in this area. The best thing you can do is accept it. You are only a virgin once, and when it is over, it is over forever. This is a hard thing to accept, I think especially for guys. At the same time, remember what I said: Everyone has been a virgin once. No big deal.

What do you do with all this awkwardness you feel because it's your first time? Be willing to communicate it with your lover (or soon-to-be lover). Hiding it is going to take a lot of effort. You'll want to scam like crazy to pretend that you are Mr. Studman and that "Loving" is your middle name. But it is hard to pretend when you are naked in front of someone and all you have is you. It is also a bad basis for intimacy to be lying about something so central to your sexuality.

• There are only two options. Either the girl is a virgin too, and then you both get to explore this for the first time together—pretty exciting stuff. Or she is not a virgin, and you can let her lead the way and introduce you to this new experience—also a pretty exciting place to be.

The more open and honest you are about what is going on, the better chance you have of being able to enjoy yourself. Also, opening yourself up is the first step toward being vulnerable, and being vulnerable is the first step toward intimacy. And to be a great lover, you must be willing to be intimate with someone else.

The Wild Thing By now

you have gotten the picture (hopefully) that making love is a continuum.

When you are the best lover, you will know

that actually having intercourse is just one possibility

during the dance.

One Course in a Feast

If you treat it like it is the end or the place where everything is heading, you are going to miss (or rush through) everything that is going on along the way. And for some couples, makin' whoopee (read: intercourse) may not be it. They may get off a lot more giving each other oral sex or watching each other masturbate.

You also will realize that in any great lovemaking, you will be stimulating each other in many ways—with your mouth, your tongue, your kisses, your words, your breath, your hands and fingers all over each other's bodies. It is not like you do steps one through nine and then you are at ten (making love) and you've reached your goal.

IN OTHER WORDS:

Intercourse, also known as screwing, banging, the old in-and-out, the horizontal watusi, doing the deep, dipping your wick, planting your seed, fucking, nailing her, boinking, nooky, under the sheets, and my favorite, making love, as I honestly feel it best describes what is (or can be) happening.

Forget Your Goal, Enjoy the Moment

In long or passionate lovemaking sessions, you will be making out for a long time and then maybe start playing with each other, massaging each other's bodies. You may be sucking her breasts or playing with her nipples with your tongue. She may be going down on you and giving you great head.

Then at a certain point you may start making love and after a while stop and go back to making out or other forms of caressing and affection. You will be using all of these different skills before, during, and after, and they are all a part of your being a great lover. My point is, don't get it in your mind that once you get inside your girlfriend this is it—or you'll have a very unsatisfied lover on your hands.

The one thing that needs to be said here again—this is really important—is that *your level of commitment needs to match this level of intimacy.* This just means you can't be as casual, aloof, or "whatever" after you are lovers with someone. You're taking on serious responsibility when you go this deep with another person.

Remember What Is Possible

Once you start being lovers with someone, and you have actually started making love, you have crossed an important threshold. The bottom line is, you could create a baby. Even if this is the furthest thing from your mind, even if you and your girlfriend are really clear that there is no way you want to have a kid now, even if you and your girl agree that she would have an abortion if anything ever happened, the bottom line is that a baby can be created, and this is why you have to take this seriously.

Birth Control Options

The first way to be responsible is to talk about it and be clear with each other about what your intention is: "I definitely do not want to have a baby," for example. The next part of your conversation should be about birth control. Here are your options:

- Rubbers (you)

- Vasectomy (you, although it is difficult to reverse and you are too young to be making this kind of permanent decision)

- Pulling out or withdrawal (when your girlfriend says, "Don't come in me," the mantra in the 1950s when birth control was under the table);

this is not an effective method.

- Rhythm, also called FAM or NFP, Fertility Awareness Method or Natural Family Planning (both of you—where you count days from the first day of her period to determine when she is fertile, on the theory that girls are fertile only in the middle of their cycles for about seven days); a lot of kids have been born because of this method—it's not effective

- Checking mucus (her—a girl checks the mucus in her vagina and notes how it changes when she ovulates, that is, when the egg is released from her ovary and pregnancy can occur); this takes a lot of attention, observation over a period of time, and commitment on both of your parts to be really careful around the fertile period—all of which point to it not being a great method for teens.

- Saliva test (her—a new test on the market, based on a girl's saliva changing during her ovulation); similar to the mucus method, again not recommended for teens.

- Birth control pills (her)

- Injections like Depo Provera, every three months, or Lunelle, once a month (her)

- Film (used with condoms—her)

- Female condoms (her)

- Spermicidal jelly or cream (used with condoms—you—or diaphragm—her)

- Diaphragm (her)

Some guys choose to wear rubbers even if their girlfriend is using another method of birth control for better protection against both pregnancy and STIs. Lots of options and lots of information.

Get the Latest Information

The information here is only cursory, and the details about birth control are important and pretty involved. So the next step here after you have declared your intent (no babies, my guess, although if you are both open to having babies, your next step should be a parenting class, and time with young babies just to get a reality check) is to declare your preferred methods of birth control. Then go to experts like Planned Parenthood or the family planning group at your local health department and get some detailed, up-to-date information.

Maybe this seems embarrassing to you, but don't worry, the people there are used to talking to teens. They don't have an attitude about your sexuality; their job is just to give you information. It's another rite of passage, going to one of these agencies with your girlfriend and really finding out what all your options are. Besides finding out what the different possibilities are for each of you, you will also learn about the risks—the likelihood of getting pregnant and how different methods can affect your own, and your partner's health.

You Can't Get 100 Percent on a Birth Control Test

No method of birth control is 100 percent foolproof. It won't do you any good to protest that she "shouldn't have" gotten pregnant because you were wearing a rubber when you came. Maybe the rubber was defective, or maybe you penetrated her before putting it on, just to see what it felt like—you're putting out sperm even before you come—or maybe it came off while you were still inside of her, or maybe you took it off after you were outside of her but then started making out and penetrated her again, and although you didn't come, there might still have been active sperm around, or maybe you forgot and were using it with an oil-based lubricant, which broke down the latex on the rubber.

Once someone is P R E G N A N T , she is pregnant and you can't argue or excuse yourself out of it. As has been said, "You can't be a little bit pregnant."

Choose Wisely

You need to know what the reality is—or the likelihood that something could happen—before you start getting sexual with someone. Different methods of birth control also have implications for the health of one or both of you. Girls and women who take the pill or get the injection(s) can gain or lose weight or have headaches, nausea, and extra bleeding, so you should know about those side effects if you are interested in that method. Rubbers, to be effective, have to be used in certain ways. Spermicides can taste bad if you are doing oral sex. And pulling out has a hundred reasons for being a bad choice. You also need to have the latest information on STIs—what tests are available, what the possible treatments are, and where you go if you think you have something, or want to find out.

I know that all this sounds like you have just cut your libido (sexual energy) off at the knees and any romantic stuff that was going on is now going to be squashed. But birth control is something you need to handle, and once you have made a decision you can then be a lot more spontaneous and romantic. You'll know what you are going to do and what your options are, and you won't have to worry about it.

It Is a Big Deal

The reason sex is such a big deal, as I said before, is that a baby is possible every time you make love. For your life, for your girlfriend's life, and for a baby's life, you cannot minimize the importance of this. Wherever you stand on the pro-life or pro-choice scale, everyone agrees that sex is not something you can be casual about. It is also a very emotional thing for both of you.

For the girl, if she does get pregnant, there is a new life inside her body. You can't (she can't) be casual about that. How she feels before she is pregnant and how she feels afterward will be two different things. Even if you agree about having an abortion, it is not a simple procedure that you just do and then go on with your life and pretend that nothing happened. It has emotional consequences—and they are big, for each of you.

I know women who had abortions twenty and thirty years ago, and none of them considers it insignificant—an abortion is that big. Even if they know it was the right thing to do, each of them talks about what a major decision it was. There is data showing that men as well feel long-term effects from abortions. An abortion can also (obviously) affect your relationship, often altering it and sometimes ending it completely. Getting pregnant is a major wake-up call, and, presuming it is not what you want to happen, it will change your sexual relationship with your lover.

Who Said Daddy?

The other (maybe even scarier or at least more long-term) possibility is that some girls will want to keep the baby. Even if you don't want to, she might want to. Some of my friends have kids out there that they never wanted to have, but they are fathers nevertheless. It is not fair for the baby. This is the most important thing. It is not the kid's decision, and growing up without a dad, or with a dad who doesn't really want to be there, leaves big scars for a child. And for you too. Even if you make the separation (and the baby is adopted or brought up by someone else, for example), some part of you will know there is a baby out there who is yours.

For those of you who do decide to have a baby, your life as you once knew it is over. In some ways (many ways) it can be a great journey, and there are a million delights with having kids, but your carefree days as a teenager are going to be gone forever. Being a parent is a tremendous amount of work. Are you ready for that?

It Started Out Loose and Innocent

The reason I bring all of this up is that I have seen this happen many times, and I know how something that was loose and fun and kind of innocent (a nice sexual episode with your girlfriend one evening) will affect you for a lot of your life. It is worth thinking about and dealing with before you crawl between the sheets.

Sex Changes Everything

On a relationship level, things also change once you get sexual. In big ways. Think about it—if you have started to make love with your girl, she is literally opening her body up to you, and you are offering up the most vulnerable part of your body to her. You can be clear with her that you are not interested in a long-term relationship or in "getting serious," she can tell you that it is fine and she doesn't want anything "heavy," but the truth is that making love is serious and heavy.

The physical act of making love says something that goes B E Y O N D your words.

Here's where boys and girls are different at times. Boys may tend to separate their bodies from their emotions. Girls may connect them up a lot more. Until they get older and have more sexual experience, girls may be less likely to view sex as casually as many boys do. I'm not saying that you will always complicate things once you become lovers, but I am saying that you cannot assume that because you have laid your cards on the table and agreed how you are going to feel that everything is clear and will be understood. It doesn't work like that.

Many guys have a fantasy of easy casual sex—and here is where it comes into direct conflict with the real world. Maybe that's why some guys end up with prostitutes—they can play out their fantasies and then walk away when their hour is up. With a real girlfriend you can have your fantasy and reality at the same time, but in order to do it you have to honor your relationship and respect your commitment to your lover. This doesn't mean you have to get married or even be together for a long time. It just means that while you are together, you pay attention to the feelings, needs, and desires of this other person, since you are involved with her. You are part of a relationship, however casual, and you need to show up to participate. Showing up just means responding to the other person and the situation at hand, in the moment it is happening.

How Do You Know She's Ready?

Now back to the basics. You have your birth control down, you are paying attention in your relationship, and things are moving toward sex.

How do you know she's ready?

You know by your girlfriend's response to you:

• How open she is to having you feel her body

• How willing she is to take off some of her clothes with you

• How wet her vagina is when you are involved in a heavy petting (read: feeling-up) session

• How she is sighing or moaning when you are giving her a hand job or head

• How eager she is to feel you up

• How clear she is verbally: "Let's make love" or "I want to get you in bed"—pretty clear

• How eager she is to take off your pants and pull you into her—again, not too confusing.

You can also try saying "Let's make love" and see what her response is:

• "Yes!" or

- "You're dreaming" or

- "We need to slow down, this is going too fast" or

- No words but she starts taking off your clothes or hers or

- "I have a headache" (the classic no).

How do you know you are ready?

- You have a hard-on bigger than the Washington Monument.

- You feel safe and connected with your girlfriend.

- You have birth control covered.

- You are emotionally prepared to take this step with her.

- Every cell in your body is saying, "Yes!"

Where You Can Be

Once you know that you want to make love, if you have any discretion, you may want to plan on where. Lots of times you will get caught in the heat of passion and be ready to do the horizontal watusi wherever you are (the back of your Toyota while you are parked at the beach watching a sunset—no problem). But there is something to be said for making this special, especially a first time with a new lover. And there is a lot to be said for not being rudely interrupted by someone's parents or siblings or having to rush butt naked into a closet to hide because the girl's dad came home unexpectedly from work or having a park ranger shine a flashlight into your tent while you are between your lover's legs and your butt is hanging out in the air. All of these things have happened, and although you get past them, it makes for much greater sex to have your encounters in a place that is safe and quiet and where you can make some sounds without being inhibited and where you won't be interrupted.

When you're a teen this sometimes takes some planning. It depends on how your parents feel about your having sex, and it depends on what your options are:

- Do you or does your girlfriend have a car?

- Is there a beach or a place in nature where you can go and be safe and private?

- Do you have enough money to rent a motel room somewhere?

- Is there a private place where you can go camping for the weekend?

- Is there a house or apartment you can stay in that you know is going to be empty for the weekend? (And is it okay with the owner of the house or apartment for you to be there?)

It isn't always easy to find the right spot, but it is worth thinking about and keeping your eyes open. A neighbor of ours told us about his son, who, when he was fourteen, spent the entire summer building this incredible tree house down by the creek. Our friend watched his son working so hard and admired how industrious he was being. Then one day in September his son asked him if he could have a sleepover with his girlfriend in the tree house, and everything became crystal clear.

It's a Natural Thing

The biggest thing you have to remember about making it is that nature is in your favor. This means that it is set up to work. People have not had books or movies or photos for thousands of years, and they have still figured out how to do the wild thing.

You are getting erections, your girlfriend is getting wet. Your bodies are working and doing exactly what they are supposed to. You can start with making out and move to a lot of touching with each other. Technically, this is called foreplay, and it is an integral part of any great lover's bag of tricks.

First Time Awareness

Part of your foreplay is paying attention to your girlfriend's vagina, to see if her hymen needs stretching. The hymen is a thin piece of skin on the inside of her vagina that can partially block the passage. (Most hymens aren't a 100 percent closure, just partial. Your girlfriend might be using tampons, but her hymen still might need some stretching.) If it hasn't been stretched, it can tear the first time a girl has intercourse, causing some bleeding. Obviously, if skin tears and bleeds, this is painful, so you will want to prevent her experiencing this kind of discomfort.

If it's her first time, the lovers-to-be can be exploring her vagina together, gently stretching the hymen. This can be part of your play together that leads up to the first time. You can also have explored together what really turns her on and gets her juicy and makes her so hot she's dying for you inside her. I heard of a certain Caribbean country where the elder women take a young bride-to-be into a private place and basically give her a spa—massages, baths, the works—and then massage her sexually, including her breasts and vulva, until she nearly faints with wanting. When she's so drugged with arousal she can barely stand, the wedding ceremony takes place. Now that is making sure someone is ready to have an ecstatic first experience!

The message here is that there doesn't have to be bleeding during a "first time"—ever—because the hymen never has to be ruptured (except in the rare case of 100 percent closure, in which case a doctor's help is advised).

Foreplay's Important

Even after her hymen has been stretched and both of you know there is enough room for you inside her, most of the time girls are not ready (physically, emotionally, or mentally) for you to just pop yourself inside them. Remember how back in the chapter titled "Girls" (page 37), I talked about how their bodies are different from yours? In general, their arousal—how the blood rushes to their genitals—happens a bit slower than your arousal. You have to respect this difference, and enjoy the process. Part of this is building up the excitement. Long, intense kissing, some fondling of her breasts, kissing her neck, blowing gently in her ear and licking her ear with your tongue, playing with her toes, massaging her thighs, giving her a full-body (not necessarily sexual) massage, reading poetry or just telling her how much she means to you—this is all foreplay, and it is increasing the passion for both of you.

For her, it is also (hopefully) turning her on and getting her natural juices (read: lubricants) flowing. If she is not wet, or if you are not getting signs that she is excited (her breathing is getting more intense, maybe she is sighing or moaning, or really coming onto you with a lot of kissing and touching, playing with your unit, getting you really excited), it just might not be happening today or right now. Sometimes you have to lighten it up.

Laughing Relaxes You Both

Laughing and humor are great in bed. Remember, this is about making it safe and building trust. Laughter is usually very safe and can open people up. Watch somebody who's uptight—if you can get them to laugh, it's hard for them to stay mad. It's the same thing in bed. Laughter and playfulness make it more normal and let both of you relax a little and let down your guard.

Not every girl wants to play the sex kitten or the vixen (aggressor). Some want to just be able to be themselves and be in bed with someone they really like and can share some intimacy with. So if that is not happening, lighten up and get a little playful. You may be surprised when the passion starts turning on after she feels safe.

Prelude to Love

If she does feel safe and takes her clothes off and jumps on top of you (hence the name "jumping your bones," another name for boinking), your body will more than likely be ready.

For many girls being on top is more fun. They can move a lot easier (and be able to stimulate themselves at the same time as they are driving you crazy), and they enjoy being in control of the rhythm of your lovemaking. It can also be an incredible turn-on for you. To have her drive you (and herself) wild while you adjust to her rhythm can be a little bit of heaven.

Once your girlfriend is on top of you, right on top of your pelvic area, with her legs spread on either side of you, nature has set things up for you to be able to make love. At first she might want to just move her vulva back and forth over your hard-on. Remember, this is stimulation for her clitoris and can help to build up her excitement. If her natural lubricants are flowing, she can be real wet and be able to move really easily. If they are not, you may want to use a water-based lubricant or even just a little saliva on your penis and/or her vagina to make things move easier.

I'm assuming at this point you have covered the issue of birth control. If you haven't, you need to stop and get the rubber on or put the spermicidal cream in, or whatever method you are going to use.

Don't wait. Passion and responsible thinking are not the best of friends, so don't assume that you can wait and make the R I G H T   D E C I S I O N as things get more intense.

Moving Inside

While your lover is moving back and forth on your member, you may just slip inside of her at some point. Or she may reach down and put you inside of her, or you may reach down and help yourself go inside of her. All are fine.

When you are inside you will find the natural movement with your body to move yourself in and out of her. There will also be a natural movement between you, which is your lovemaking dance. Going slow, going fast, coming out of her and then going back in—all are part of it.

Once you are inside, you may feel like you are going to come and don't want to yet. For many guys, coming is the end of their lovemaking, and having things go on for a while can prolong the pleasure and give the girl time to build to an orgasm. The release of coming is great—and so are the excitement and anticipation that build up to it—so great lovers often try to really get into the loving and prolong their enjoyment. You may want to pull yourself out and just wait for a while if you need to slow yourself down a little. Go back to kissing or massaging her or caressing her body to get her closer to orgasm too. It is likely that you will be ready to come first. It is also likely that she will want you to pay attention to her clitoris with your hand, fingers, mouth, lips, tongue, or penis to get her ready to orgasm.

Change the Pace

When you are first starting to have sex, being inside your lover for a long time may be too much for you to be able to control (you're going to want to come). So go back and forth, being inside her and then pulling yourself out. This will help you gain more control. For some guys switching in and out is a complete turn-on, so don't get stuck if you need to change the pace. Also remember that your entire body is involved, not just your thing. Use your hands, your eyes, your toes, your mouth as part of your lovemaking. It is all about touch and being present with your lover.

Each Position Changes Your Experience

You can also change positions. There is the standard, girl lying on her back with legs spread, boy on top, also called the missionary position. Even in this position, though, you can be creative. Your girlfriend can hold onto her thighs and bring them back toward her body, or she can have her legs straight up in the air, or she can wrap them all the way around you. Each of these positions will feel different, and you will find some you enjoy more than others. Each will stimulate different parts of you and your lover, so talk to each other and see which ones each of you likes.

Try switching positions. You can enter your lover from behind. She can be up on all fours, and you can come in from behind her (doggie style).

She can also lie on her back, keeping one leg flat on the bed and bending the knee that is closer to you, while you are on your side facing her, your bottom leg resting under her straight leg and your upper leg resting over that same leg, so that her bent knee rests on your upper leg. In this position, you can easily enter your girlfriend, and it offers some great opportunity for you (and her) to stimulate her clitoris and for both of you to move easily. This can be very erotic.

The Bed Is Only One Place

Another thing to think about besides different positions is different places. Try moving to the edge of the bed. Your lover can be sitting on the edge of the bed with her feet over the side, and you can be standing up right next to her with her legs wrapped around you.

You can also pick her up (depending on how strong you are and how small or big she is) and carry her around while you are still inside of her, to another place on the bed or to the floor or maybe a chair.

If you have an easy chair or a couch, you can get into great positions on either.

Try standing up with one of you against a wall. You may want a chair or table close by so your girlfriend can use it to prop her leg on. It will make it easier for you to come inside of her.

Then there are "water sports." Showers, bathtubs, hot tubs, and pools (depending on the temperature of the water) can all be great places to be sexual. If you have enough room, you can move around weightlessly in water and it can be very sensual. You will also see that gravity sometimes works to your advantage, so you are having a different experience when you are in a different medium. Just feeling water around you in a shower or a tub can be very sexual and really arousing. Soaping each other can also be part of your lovemaking. Be careful of soap, though. It can let you move on each other really easily, which is so sensual, but if you get it in the opening in your penis, or your girlfriend gets it in her vulva, it can really burn.

You get to be creative with where you make love. Keep in mind, though, that you both have to feel comfortable with it. Your girlfriend might want to keep making love on your bed or hers, or she might want to experiment and explore different options. To be the best lover, you just need to be open to various possibilities and sensitive to how your lover is responding.

Surprises and Spontaneity

When you are the best lover, you approach s e x

with the a w a r e n e s s that you and your lover are entering

a great mystery together. Lovemaking is the part of life that connects us

to both the p h y s i c a l and the s p i r i t u a l aspects of life.

Sounds pretty esoteric and out there, huh? Really, it doesn't have to be.

It's a matter of tuning in to y o u r i n t u i t i o n .

Tuning In to Your Intuition

Intuition is the part of us that knows more than our conscious mind knows. Whether you call it your intuition or higher self or conscience, it is a part of us that everyone has, so everyone also has access to the information it provides. We can grow in our ability to use it, though. The more you pay attention to it, the more in touch with it you become.

Here are some questions that might help you get in touch with your intuition:

• What's your inner voice saying is the right thing to do?

• How does this situation feel? Is it safe? Are you uncomfortable? Is there a sense of excitement?

• Are you willing to pay attention to your intuition even if it is telling you something you may not want to hear?

The more you honor your intuition, the clearer the voice will get. You will get more information, not necessarily because more is coming to you, but just because you are paying more attention to it. It is like using your radio or your satellite dish—the information is always there, you are just fine-tuning your receptors to pick it up.

The Intuitive Lover

The more intuitive you become, the greater of a lover you will be. Why? Because you will be more aware of the magic and mystery in sex, and so you will be able to take advantage of them to become more spontaneous and to surprise your lover. Spontaneity and surprise are two big tricks of the best lover.

Whenever you make love—whether it's the first time or the thousandth time with the same lover—she will really appreciate it if you show creativity and passion in your affections. Nobody wants a lover who is just going through the motions. And nobody—ever—wants a lover who is just following a script. The one habit that keeps many people—and I think especially boys—from being great lovers is the tendency to go for the big O, to focus all their attention on orgasm.

Making love is about enjoying the whole process, not just going for the final destination. When you are in bed with someone, it's not just about where you're going, it's also about all the detours you make together to get there. It's the trip you are taking coming home from a skiing vacation when you decide to take a side road to a hot springs you have heard about, and a half hour later after a bumpy road you are soaking in these gorgeous natural springs looking up at the mountains. And when you are a really great lover, you will enjoy the hot springs as much as reaching home base. Why? Because on the road to the hot springs, anything can happen. You don't know what you will encounter along the way, you don't know how it will be when you get there. You're just taking it step-by-step, keeping your eyes wide open as you go.

When you're making love and you get that same anything-can-happen feeling, it adds a rush of passion that turns scripted sex into magical sex. But to enjoy surprises, you have to be present in the moment. Being spontaneous is about being open to things happening that you never could have planned. At the moment you are surprised, you can either resist the surprise because it wasn't what you were planning, or you can surrender to it and have a great time.

People who are the best lovers often set up a scene to surprise their lover and to remind themselves to enjoy the moment. Here are some examples of lovers who enjoyed surprises and allowed the magic to happen.

Walking into a Western Movie

I have friends who were getting together over a period of months, slowly building up to a sexual relationship. They lived in separate states, so it was a few weeks in between when they would see each other. Well, one weekend my friend, Mark, was going up to see Diane, and she had planned for them to go to a dinner party that night. He picked her up, and on the way over to the party, she said she had forgotten something and asked if they could just drive by her studio. She was an actress and also taught classes out of her studio. When they drove up in front of her studio, she said she would just be a minute, so he waited outside in the car. After about five minutes she still had not returned, so he went over to the door of her studio and asked if she was okay. She shouted yes, but could he come in and help her with something. He wandered in, and the entire studio was set up as a scene from a western movie. The lights were low, it looked like a smoky barroom, and she was dressed up as a scantily dressed barmaid. Mark was totally surprised and realized he was in the middle of a drama. He immediately began playing along as Diane seduced him and made passionate love to him on the couch she had set up in the middle of the barroom. Yippee-yi-yo!

Be Willing to Change Plans

The thing about surprises, especially when sexual feelings are involved, is that you have to be flexible and willing to change. If your girlfriend or you are definitely not in the mood to be the barmaid or the cowboy on this particular night, it may not work, so have a fallback plan. Maybe you can switch to reading her poetry (cowboy poetry in this case), and see how things progress.

The Red Shirt

One of my young friends, Chas, planned a great surprise for his
girlfriend, Linda. She was going away, and he invited her over to his
house. When she got there, at the foot of the door was an envelope with
a big letter L on it and a single rose next to it and a candle burning.
When she opened up the envelope she found a beautiful poem about her
that began with the letter L. At the end of the poem, he had written,
"Come on in." She went through the front door, and on the far side of
the room, on a side table, she saw another envelope with a candle next
to it and a rose. This envelope had the letter I and another poem inside
that began with I, again about Linda and how much Chas liked her. She
proceeded through the house, finding the envelopes marked N and D,
each with a candle and a rose next to it. Finally, she ended up in Chas's
room, where she found the A envelope, a candle, and a whole bouquet
of red roses. And there was Chas, dressed in a red shirt, the same shirt
Linda had had a dream about Chas in (and told him about) only a week
before. They ended the evening with a romantic candlelight dinner that
Chas had completely prepared himself.

Surprising Yourself to Remember

Surprises can also shift a relationship that has gotten stuck or maybe is in
too much of a routine. The danger with anything that goes on for a while
is that you (or your lover) can start taking it for granted, and nobody
likes to be taken for granted. Once you do that, you stop seeing the
person for who they are. You tend to box them in to a certain set of
expectations (for good or bad), and they're likely to feel stifled and
confined. A nice surprise every now and then can let you both remember
why you were attracted to each other in the first place. A surprise that

my girlfriend Patty once planned helped our lovemaking come alive again.

The Wood Nymph

Patty and I were out on a hike some years ago, all the way back in the mountains, far off the regular trail. Patty had grown up in this area and was showing me some great little creeks and swimming holes that she had known as a kid. Down at a swimming hole, we had taken off our clothes and were splashing around, jumping off a rock on the side of the hole and enjoying playing. For a while I was just floating on my back, closing my eyes and thinking about what a gorgeous day it was.

When I opened my eyes Patty was gone. I thought maybe she had gone off to pee, but after a few minutes she was still gone, so I started calling her. Finally I heard her voice, off in the distance, singing, so I got on some clothes and started following it. She wasn't answering my calls, but the singing was definitely her voice, so I kept going toward the sound. Five minutes later I was still hiking up the mountain but could no longer hear her voice. Then I heard some twigs snapping and looked off to the side to catch sight of someone dashing off behind one of the big oak trees. I ran up, panting and a little out of breath, to discover Patty the wood nymph, in a sheer gauze skirt and top, with nothing on underneath, waiting for me next to this fairy palace she had set up with a bed (a blanket she had brought for our supposed picnic), some wildflowers, and a candle with incense burning next to it. She had this sweet smile on her face, and I knew that the afternoon was about to get even better. Just the fact that someone would have put that much thought into surprising me, in addition to wanting to make love with me, was pretty special—a great treat.

Spontaneous Love

Sometimes being spontaneous means taking advantage of a moment that neither of you has planned. What happens turns out to be a surprise for both of you. If you thought about it too long, you might talk yourself out of it, but in the right situation at the right time, you just go for it and abandon your fears.

Hospital Visit

My friend Jason was once hospitalized with a badly broken leg. He had been laid up for six weeks and was going a little stir-crazy in the hospital. One day his girlfriend, Debbie, came to visit him, like she had been doing every few days. She was a nurse and worked the late-night shift, so it was usually late afternoon by the time she came by.

Jason was watching TV when Debbie came in, and he started talking about how miserable he was and frustrated that it would still be another two weeks before he would be able to get out and how he was just waiting for the next set of pain meds, which were still an hour away.

Debbie got up, closed the door to the hallway, and pulled the screen around his bed. Jason started asking, "What are you doing?" but when she took off her panties and carefully climbed on top of the bed, straddling him, he just shut up. Debbie proceeded to make love to him in the middle of his boring hospital afternoon. That's spontaneity.

The 1st to 42nd Floors

I remember once falling in love at a business event years ago and getting in the elevator with this woman I had met, anticipating that we would likely be in my room soon and hopefully be making love. But between the 1st and 42nd floors, we were all over each other. We didn't do the wild thing in the elevator, but we did everything else. By the time we reached the 42nd floor (thankful that it hadn't stopped to pick up anyone else), I was exhausted, had a hard-on bigger than the Empire State Building, and we tumbled out of the elevator and stumbled to my room to enjoy the rest of the night together.

The Universe Conspires

Spontaneity has to be consensual—you both have to agree. It takes a little magic. It is that moment when you look at each other and can feel the energy between you. You know you are both thinking the same thing, and the feeling in the air is palpable. You will know inside of you that anything is possible at that moment.

When you can be spontaneous, you throw caution to the wind and give in to the magic that is between you. Well, maybe not all caution—you don't want to embarrass yourselves—but at a moment like this the universe is giving you a window of opportunity to enjoy something that normally you would never consider. After you do, you will always remember it, and an elevator may never look the same again.

Only One Rule

Only one thing to remember with spontaneity: even in the middle of the moment, you don't want to (read: can't) throw away your sense of responsibility. This means birth control.

You can be very spontaneous and passionate and wild, but you still have to remember to be clear that at least one of you is going to be responsible for practicing birth control and safe sex. Having babies or getting an STI is anything but spontaneous; don't let something wild and innocent get much more complicated because you let go of everything in the heat of the moment. Carry a rubber with you all the time, even if you are not planning on having anything happen, and then you won't have to worry.

If you don't, I will tell you right now that in the heat of passion, 99 percent of people will go ahead and have sex even if it is risky. Once you get really turned on with someone, you're not likely to listen to your rational mind when it tells you to stop and say, "Well, we really shouldn't do this right now, it's not safe." More than likely, every cell in your body will be screaming, "Don't worry, have a good time, we will be fine." Famous last words!

Responsibility We've talked a lot

already about how being a lover and being responsible

go hand in hand. Listen to the word: responsible.

It means "able to respond."

If you are not able to respond, you will not be a great lover.

Responsibility is as simple —and as hard—as

showing up in the moment.

The same quality that leads you to spontaneous, surprising sex helps you be responsible to your partner throughout your time together. You need to be able to pick up on what is going on in the moment and respond to it appropriately. If you can't, you'll be a one-trick pony. You might know how to have sex, but that is light-years away from being the best lover.

It's the Species Thing

It's worth repeating: there is a real potential for a baby to be born every time you make love. That is what is driving this whole thing. Even if you are doing it for fun and pleasure, the bigger picture is that it was set up to keep the species (us) going.

Nature has a strong instinct for survival, and that is why pleasure is connected with making love. Think about it—if every time you made love it was like going to the dentist, not many people would get born. But instead there is a big payoff when you make love, which motivates people to keep doing it. It's pleasurable. It feels great.

Because babies are the bottom line, and because teenagers usually do not want to become parents or throw away their youth and freedom at the age of fifteen (or thirteen or eighteen or whenever), before you even start, you have your first opportunity to be responsible. This means, simply, not sticking your head in the sand. The three things you cannot do are:

• Pretend this is not happening

• Pretend you don't have to deal with it

• Pretend that if you don't do anything it will take care of itself and everything will be okay (and we will all live happily ever after)

It doesn't work that way. Talk to your parents. Talk to people who had babies when they were teenagers. Talk to friends of your folks, who had their fourth child when they got wild one night. This happens all the time. People have babies when they were not planning to or were not ready. At best they have the grace to accept this and are willing to raise a baby. At worst they end up aborting the baby, having the baby and giving it up for adoption, or raising a child that they are not really prepared for emotionally, financially, or spiritually.

Showing Up for the Good and for the Tough

It's easy to be responsible when things are going great. Sheer ecstasy? No problem, you think—I can handle that! The real test is when things don't always go right. Can you show up for the agony as well? We all know what the ecstasy is—the making love, the pleasure of sharing your body with someone else who is doing the same. The other possibility is what can come next—the "morning after." Some of the not-fun things are pretty simple, like a yeast infection, and some are a major deal, like when your girlfriend phones and tells you she is pregnant (yikes). If your girlfriend calls and tells you she is sore from a wild night of passionate sex, the response is *not*:

- "Big deal"

- "Not my problem"

- "So deal with it"

- "Huh?"

- (silent man)

- Not saying anything but thinking, "Wow, am I a major stud or what?"

All of these responses fall into the "clueless" category, with a touch of "insensitive" and "jerk" thrown in. All except the last one, which definitely falls into the "total worthless loser" category. The person in the last one will definitely never be a great lover.

Hurting another person, especially someone who has shared her body with you, is not something you want to do—ever.

It is not that hard to show up. Showing up just means that you acknowledge that something is going on and that you had something to do with it and that you choose to deal with it. Showing up for a yeast infection might mean that you go on the Internet and look up what causes yeast infections, what the options are for dealing with them, and how to prevent them. Your girlfriend may not want you to help with her yeast infection, even by providing information; it may just be too private for her. But at least you have the information.

The Blue-Dot Phone Call

Now we come to the phone call that every guy is petrified of getting at some point in his life. It is the "I missed my period" or "I just got a blue dot on an EPT (early pregnancy test)" call. You suddenly realize that she is not talking about something that happened in grammar class and that the color blue has just lost all appeal for you, even though two minutes ago you had no idea what it meant. You are now in a position of having to deal with a major life issue. You are allowed to be scared here. That is normal. Here are some responses you do not want to make:

- You just can't run and hide or abandon your girlfriend to deal with it or act helpless and like you have no idea how this could have happened.

- You can't push this on her with "I thought you were dealing with the birth control."

- You also can be upset, but it is more appropriate to talk to someone you trust then to dump your feelings on your girlfriend. Remember, this is her body that is affected. She *has to* deal with this.

- It is also not okay for you to say, "This is going to mess up my whole life. How could you do this to me?"

- Insults are also completely out of line, like, "Oh, how could you be so stupid to let this happen?"

What you do have to do is be there with her through this and do the right thing. Go forward step by step with your girlfriend, and be a man.

Q u e s t i o n : Who is going to tell her parents?

C l u e : Both of you.

Q u e s t i o n : Who is going to tell your parents?

C l u e : Both of you.

Even if her parents are furious with you, they will respect you (maybe not now but at some point in the future) for standing by her. She will also respect you, and you will end up respecting you. Even if this relationship is over, or maybe it was never even happening, when you are present there with her and do the right thing, you will be able to look back and stand tall, knowing you were honorable.

Taking Equal Responsibility

If she has to go to a doctor to get checked, you should say, "I am going with you." If she says she would rather have her girlfriend go, that is okay, but at least let her know where you are, and check with her before and after to do your part. Maybe make her a meal she likes for when she gets back, or have some flowers with a nice note waiting for her.

There were two of you having sex, and so two of you need to be present in dealing with any consequences. Leaving it to the girl to deal with it because it is her body just gives guys the worst rap in the world—that we really are worthless and not willing to take any responsibility. You've got to be better than that. If she and you end up deciding to have an abortion, you have to go through that together too.

Some guys turn flaky at this point. I call it the "it's not my problem response"—when the going gets tough, you cut out. Unfortunately in our culture, there aren't a lot of great role models for guys or men to do anything else. We have a lot of images of the tough man defending his family, but few images show men sharing responsibility in real-life situations. In our relationships with girls and women, we have one of the greatest opportunities to figure out life's dramas together. The path I am suggesting means that even if it is scary or uncomfortable and the going is tough, you choose to hang in and go through it. Now that is worthy of a long-term relationship or friendship or at least looking back and saying, "Wow, that guy was a stand-up guy, someone with integrity." Most important, that is someone you can be proud of—you.

Being Present in Love

The final note on responsibility is maybe the hardest part. It's about being present while you are actually making love with someone. This is also one of the greatest tools for being the best lover.

Being present while you are being lovers is about noticing what is going on and being willing to speak up if something's not quite right. This is not easy. You are already feeling vulnerable. Your whole self is just hanging out there. You are literally naked physically, and now you also have to reveal what is going on inside too. This is so hard, in fact, that even many adults chicken out—to their loss.

Did You Say Something?

The truth here is that speaking up when you are uncomfortable is the key to intimacy—just as much as speaking up when things are going well. Intimacy is about letting another person know the good and the bad about what is going on. It can start with sharing some poem with her that reveals a very sensitive part of yourself. That may be challenging, but at least it is doable. But try sharing information about something you are really embarrassed or maybe even ashamed about—now that is tough.

- Situation: Maybe you can't get hard and your girlfriend is ready for passionate sex.

- Response: Are you going to say, "Sorry," and just shrug your shoulders or turn over and go to sleep?

- Situation: What if it is obvious that your girlfriend didn't climax when you were making love?

- Response: Should you say something or wait for her to bring it up?

- Situation: How about if you have a painful aching from not coming after you've have had some passionate foreplay but didn't get to ejaculate and are limping around the next day?

- Response: Do you pretend you feel fine?

- Situation: Or what if she is closing her eyes and not looking at you while you were making love?

- Response: Do you just assume it doesn't matter?

- Situation: Say she calls out someone else's name in the middle of your having sex.

- Response: Do you pretend that didn't happen or that you heard some thing else?

Finding Wisdom

This is really hard stuff to talk about. It will also get harder as you get older if you get in the habit of not talking about it. But it will get easier if you practice dealing with it and becoming comfortable with it. If you want to be the best lover, you have no choice: you have to talk about it. This is just being present.

You may have no clue about whether this is a big deal or a minor deal, but you decide that you are going to work on it. And something about being willing to deal with it can also bring you the strength, courage, and wisdom you will need.

A Knight at King Arthur's Court

It is like being a knight at King Arthur's court. You are being asked to do the noble thing. There is a dragon to slay, and you may have no idea how to slay that dragon, but your conviction as a knight is that you are going to go out there and show up to deal with it. You might even be scared. That's okay. You can be scared and still decide to go through with it.

You may get more scared by not dealing with a problem than by confronting the reality. When there is a problem, we tend to anticipate the worst. But in the moment of reality, as the dragon comes to you, you will find your courage.

A Knight in the Bedroom

You are brave when you notice something uncomfortable and you say something about it. You're also honoring the fact that you are in a sexual relationship with someone by doing this. The fact is, your girlfriend is involved too. She might be uncomfortable about the same thing. Your fear is that she will laugh at you or be disgusted, but the truth is that everyone has fears and embarrassments, and once you reveal what you see or feel is going on, you open the door for the other person to do the same. This is the start of intimacy.

Talking about a problem also takes a big weight off both your shoulders. Hiding that stuff or pretending it isn't happening takes a lot of effort. It is much easier to deal with problems (read: find solutions to them) once things are out in the open. You also may find that your lover has some information and actually wants to help you overcome some problem. She may have a secret or two about how to help you not come too quickly or how to get you hard when your unit is limp and flaccid. She may also be a little embarrassed, but also a little touched, that you want to make sure she gets off (read: orgasm) too.

It is a big risk being this responsible. It may not always be received positively. Some people will have more invested in keeping up the façade or pretending nothing uncomfortable is going on. You just have to trust that bringing it up is the right thing to do. You are at least honoring your own perceptions and your own insights. You are also being present for your lover on the most real level. And this is always a key to being the best lover. It really is the only opportunity we have to grow and open up to the magic.

Fun and Change

I'll tell you why I am saving fun and change until almost the end

—they are the two things that people tend to forget.

Guys and girls can be having a great time,

laughing and being really playful with each other,

but when they get into bed, this performance thing

takes over and everyone forgets to play.   It's a big mistake.

Laughing into Passion

Laughing and playing with your lover are integral to being the best lover. It is not all about who can make love the longest or in the most positions. It is about letting the walls down and being able to be yourself. The passion will come. The intense, wild animal feelings will be there—they are inherent in each of us. But the lighter, humorous part is essential too. Before and after and in the middle of making love, you need to be able to look at each other sometimes and laugh. It is a release too. It reveals the innocence.

Being playful is probably a big part of why you enjoy each other's company. Taking yourself too seriously is only a recipe for being stuck. Being able to laugh breaks things up. It can let you see a new perspective, and it is very romantic while you are in bed with someone. I am not talking about making a joke out of your loving or the kind of humor that is at someone else's expense or is unkind. I am talking about the playfulness that lets you each giggle and smile and enjoy that here you are making great love, and you still like each other at the same time.

Life Is Change

I mentioned being stuck as a consequence of being too rigid or too stiff. Well, being stuck can also happen from just getting into a routine or from being with someone for a while. Change is a natural part of life. The seasons change, days flow into nights, the moon goes through phases. It is all constantly shifting. But we humans like to get into a groove and then just keep playing the same record over and over.

In relationships this can be deadly. People do not stay the same. Over any period of time, we are all going to be experiencing different things. You have to be able to check in with the person you are being lovers with and see where she is at any moment. Don't assume she's the same as she was last week. Assuming just puts people in a box, and it means you are not paying attention to who they are right now.

Stay Flexible

Part of being a great lover is always being flexible. You need to be strong like an oak tree, with deep roots (your values and honesty and integrity) and have flexible branches that can bend without breaking in a strong wind (being able to change when the situation warrants it). You might start the evening thinking you are going to have wild passionate sex and then realize that what your girlfriend really needs is to talk, and a walk in the park may be more appropriate. This is flexibility. Being able to move and change and adapt are the keys to being the best lover.

You can be flexible in when you make love. If you always make love at night, try making love first thing in the morning. Or wake your lover up in the middle of the night—that can be incredible too. Or try the middle of the afternoon if you want to change the entire day.

Or try variations in where you make love. You may be used to it always being in your bed. Well, try it outdoors, at the beach or on a mountaintop. Or how about a hotel room or a pool or shower? Try being sexual when you have to hide it, like when you are out at a restaurant with your hands under the table. I knew a girl once who loved going to a restaurant with no panties on and then taking her lover's hand during the dinner and leading him in to touch her while they were laughing or talking over their meal.

The only limitation here is your own creativity. Change is your tool, and your imagination is the door that will lead you into so many new possibilities. Each time you discover a new one, you will get a smile on your face and realize that a whole new possibility has opened up that you never thought of before.

Love

I said before that making love was quite a literal description of having sex. I was being serious. It is also the reason why I am saving this for last. It is the most important thing you need to know.

All You Need

The Beatles said, "All You Need Is Love," and although there might be a few other pieces to making a full life (a passion, work, dear friends, family, to name a few), what they nailed was the one thing at the center. Without love it is hard to make sense out of much in this life. With love, everything falls into place. It doesn't solve every problem, but it does make every problem worth solving.

The Beast and Beyond

Making love happens on two major levels. The first level might be called the animal level—tapping into the beasts that we are at a deep level and letting them come out and play. This is the sex that I will call wild, abandoned, uninhibited sex. Finding the beast can lead you to a lot of energy and passion.

This is the "wild man" and "wild woman" mode, where you really get in touch with your instinctive sexuality and break free of the constraints. To be a great lover, it is important to get to this place. Making love is not composed and demure or refined. It is wild and impulsive and somewhat abandoned. You can't be a great lover by reading a book and just using your intellect to analyze what to do. At some point you have to let go, see what you are feeling, see what your lover is desiring, and take a chance.

The cautionary note here is that if you get too much into being wild, you might cross over a boundary. If you start biting your lover in your moment of abandon, you may bite too hard and get a loud and angry "ouch" or "you're hurting me" from a shocked girlfriend who is worried that you just went off the deep end. A hickey (the bruise mark, usually a little black and blue) on your or her neck after a night of intense making out can be the telltale sign that makes you smile to remember the wild abandonment or feel embarrassed about and want to hide. So there is a balance here. You may start "talking dirty" to your girlfriend, saying, "I want to get laid," and it may be a total turn-off for her. Having her say "I want you inside me now" may totally excite you. And it may not, or it may change over time and from person to person. Some girls may find that kind of language repulsive and offensive, and you have to respect that. You want to go wild while at the same time remembering to respect where your lover is at as well.

The Lover

But there is another mood in sex that takes us from physical instinct into the territory of heart and soul. This is where sex becomes making love. When you become connected to another person at that level—physically, emotionally, and mentally connected—when you have completely revealed yourself to someone else, shown her all that you are, when you are wanting to make that other person completely happy and are willing to totally give yourself to do that, when your heart is open and bursting with joy, you are literally making love. You are creating love at that moment.

The magic happens when you are in the present moment—when all of your fears are gone, when you are not thinking about the past or the future—when you are just completely with that other person, the two of you in each other's arms, when you can see yourself in your lover's eyes. The feeling in the air at that moment is quite palpable.

If you are acting at all times out of love, if you are honoring your lover and yourself, if you are holding that up as your highest ideal, you will be the best lover, because the most important tool of all, to be the best lover, is always your heart.

The End

Notes

1. Joni Mitchell, "Come In From The Cold," from "Night Ride Home," Geffen Records, 1991. Page 60.

2. Joni Mitchell, "Come In From The Cold," from "Night Ride Home," Geffen Records, 1991. Page 60-61.

3. Respect, Aretha Franklin, from "I've Never Loved A Man The Way I Love You," Atlantic & Atco Remasters, 1967. Page 90.

Appendix

The Sex Talk

"Do you know any other names for erections?" I ask my son as he is lying next to me on our bed. He says, "Boners." I say, "Stiffies, woodies, chubbies." I tell him the quote from Mae West: "Is that a gun in your pocket, or are you just happy to see me?" I recount embarrassing scenes from my teenage years, when I would get a huge hard-on while in a bathing suit and then not be able to move. I expose myself through vulnerable stories to him. I try to make it fun. I also seek, through questions I ask, to be clear that there is a lot he does not know.

We are in the middle of our Sex Talk. We always do our sessions lying down on our backs, side by side, either on my bed or outside in the hammock. We are always alone and undisturbed. I don't answer the phone or let anything else distract us. The other kids know they can't bother us, and the door stays closed. Lying together is perfect, kind of like we are cuddling, and it is a nice way to approach this subject. He doesn't feel like I am staring at him. He is able to have his own reactions. I think that sitting at a table would be too much like a lecture, and we would lose a lot of the connection we are gaining. We are doing something together rather then me just telling him something.

The closeness of our setting is opening the door for me to ask him some intimate questions: "Have you had a wet dream?" "Have you seen a rubber?" "Have you tried putting one on?" "Have you smoked?" I let him know that he is going to have some of these experiences and I want him to have the right information. I also use it as an entree into letting him know that he can tell me or choose to have it be private the first time he masturbates and that this is a rite of passage. If he wants to I will honor him in some way, or he can just keep it to himself; it is his choice.

Our Sex Talk started a few weeks before my son's thirteenth birthday, when I announced to him that we were going to have the conversation. Big surprise, he tried to do the same thing I had done as a teenager—slough it off. When I was thirteen, one day around the dining room table, at a probably prearranged moment, my mom quickly disappeared into the kitchen and my dad awkwardly and uncomfortably said, "I want to talk with you about sex." It was the conversation I had been dreading for the past year. Now here it was. We never talked about these kinds of things. In fact, we never talked about anything too deep or real. I immediately retorted, "Well, what do you want to know?" It was a line I had planned for months. It worked.

Now my son, not having given this as much thought as I did, tries a simple, "No, I don't want to." Unfortunately for him, I am more persistent than my dad. Then he tries reason: "But I read the book already." I feel my resistance wane. The knot in my stomach cinches tighter, and my breaths grow shorter. At this moment the easiest thing in the world would be to acquiesce. I only push through because I have made a commitment to face things I don't want to face in my life. This one is a glaring sign flashing neon, and I know I have to follow it.

This moment started a year ago when my son turned twelve and I came up with a list of things I needed to talk with him about—drugs, alcohol, smoking, and, yes, sex. The ones I didn't think about were honesty (lying), keeping your commitments, responsibility, doing the right thing, finding your destiny, finding a group with your same interests—and the list keeps growing.

This is the sticky stuff, the things every father is supposed to talk about but would rather not. The truth is that most of my generation's dads never talked about this stuff; they were a combination of too busy and too uncomfortable with the subject matter. Some of it they had little or no experience with, like drugs. And sex was something you just picked up along the way, kind of figured out for yourself. So my friends and I had no map of where we were going and no models to work from.

Once I had my list, though, I put off doing much about it. Well, I found people in a drug rehabilitation program for teens to come give a talk to my son's class, and I got the American Lung Association to show the kids what lungs filled with tar looked like, and I located another group involved with teen alcoholism to open a dialogue with the kids in his group. But the big one, sex, I kept putting off.

As I watched the months go by, I had to admit how scary and uncomfortable this was for me. It is uncomfortable for most dads, and parents in general, which is why they avoid it or don't do it or hope the school will take care of it or assume their kids know what they need to— or will learn it from friends—or throw their kids a book to fulfill their parental responsibility.

Some friends, when I ask if they have had the Sex Talk with their sons, nervously laugh and say, "Well, I'm sure they know." But what can they know? What can most boys who are twelve or thirteen know? Maybe the mechanics—but that's not at all what sex is about, or it's only a small part. The depth comes from experience and having different lovers or being with the same lover for long enough to really explore this realm and realizing what works and what doesn't. And this is what, I know— way back deep inside, behind a whole lot of discomfort—we have to talk about.

My discomfort surprises me. After all, I was part of the sexual revolution.

My coming of age began in the sixties, when taboos were broken, old rules changed. "Free love" meant that I would end up making love with friends or women I knew, just because there was a familiarity or a spark and we were open to experimenting. It was great, it was exciting—and now I realize I was pretty clueless. We had sex, but mostly we didn't talk about sex. We experimented but mostly didn't check in with our partners about what felt good. I listened for the moans but was scared to talk in more depth. I loved the freedom but hoped my girlfriends took responsibility for not getting pregnant. So here I am, fifty years old, revisiting my old, familiar discomfort about sex. Can I grow through it this time?

The book my son says he has read is what we choose as our guide; it is the only guide we have. My wife found the book on a trip to northern California, and it gives us just enough structure to know where to start. It is comprehensive, presents the material in a straightforward manner, starting with the meaning of the words, and uses cartoons for graphic illustrations. I think actual pictures would be too much for my son. The cartoons are safe. They are also explicit enough to give him all of the information he needs. They are a perfect entry point. The book also makes sure that I won't leave anything out.

It also provides some comic relief. Two cartoon characters are engaged in an ongoing dialogue. Early on, my son and I decide that he will be one character and I will be the other. So every time we come to these characters I read the one part and my son reads the other. My son's character is always saying things like, "Do we have to talk about this?" We crack up.

The thoroughness in our approach is both good and bad. Good in reminding me how many issues are involved. Bad in realizing this is going to take much longer than I had thought. Before I know it, summer is upon us, and it isn't until the fall that we resume again. We end up spending six one- to two -hour sessions on this, over about six months. Now I think my initial idea of a one- to two-hour Sex Talk was probably just more evidence of how uncomfortable I am with the subject and how I wanted to just get through it.

The truth, as I come to realize it, is that this talk isn't just about making love or masturbating. It's important to cover birth control, relationships, babies, responsibility, abortion, STIs, and even anatomy. Also, part of what we are doing is just getting comfortable talking about the subject. This takes time. My son needs to hear me say "penis," "vagina," "breasts," "sexual intercourse," "blow job," "come," and "hard-on" a number of times before we both get over our embarrassment. So the time is actually part of the message. We have to go through it. It's a dialogue.

The discussion is as important as the information. I begin to realize that I am opening the door for my son to be able to come to me in the future when he starts making love and is coming too quickly and wants advice. We get that specific. I want him to know that it's just information and that, in addition to his friends or books, I am there to help him.

What I get in going through the Sex Talk with my son is the process—sharing my own experiences when I was thirteen, how I fumbled, mistakes I made, how I really didn't know but had to pretend I knew, and what I learned. We are learning to talk about sex with each other, and our relationship grows in a big way. It's not just about sex, it's about both of us revealing what we don't know. We are becoming vulnerable with each other. It is so scary that often my chest starts to tighten and my heart to race. And then at some point it shifts, and we are just two guys hanging out, talking about the real stuff in life. We have crossed an important threshold. My son realizes that now everything is open for discussion and I am willing to relate to him on a different level. The shock of it takes some getting used to—for each of us. We are trying on new clothes and need to get comfortable in them.

Our Sex Talk has become a rite of passage, for both of us. I am passing along some basic information to my son, as people have done for centuries, about a few things I have found that work in this life. The eldership is being reestablished, a father transmitting to his son information that is actually valuable and valued and that helps to make his journey a little easier.

A few months later, when my son gets a girlfriend older than he is (she is a senior and he a freshman), I think of a whole new set of issues that we need to talk about. We haven't yet covered pleasuring a woman or emotional intimacy, for instance. And how will I tell him about getting your heart broken? Do I open the possibility of breaking up with someone and still being friends because, as much as it hurts, you love this person so much that nothing else makes sense? How far do I go in explaining techniques of oral sex? Do I tell him about making in love in the shower, in nature, or on your favorite overstuffed chair?

Suddenly I know that the door I have opened leads to a much bigger room than I ever suspected. There is so much he doesn't know. There is also so much I don't know. We are in uncharted territory again. Only now I trust that we will find our way, together.

Index

The Companion Book for
"How to Be the Best Lover
A Guide for Teenage Boys"

First Love
Remembrances

Howard B. Schiffer

This is the "other half of the conversation", what you always wanted to know ~ how it really was for teenagers the first time they had sex, the first time they made love, and their first romances. Over 50 stories from people around the world!

www.heartfullovingpress.com or
www.firstloveremembrances.com

Read this *before* you read any other parenting book!
This book gives you the basics; what you need
to know to keep your family in great shape.
A primer in heart centered parenting!

HOW TO BE A FAMILY
The Operating Manual

Howard B. Schiffer

*With every other thing in life from your cell phone
to your computer, you get an instruction manual. Yet people
start having children virtually clueless. "How to Be a Family"
is the basic operating manual, the simple instructions and
wisdom of what it takes to raise kids in a heart centered
environment and to keep your family together, happy, healthy
and thriving.*

www.heartfullovingpress.com or
www.firstloverembrances.com

Easy Order Form

Fax orders: (805) 687 3042
E-Mail orders: orders@heartfullovingpress.com
Postal orders: Heartful Loving Press, PO Box 30041, Santa Barbara, CA 93130, USA
On Line orders: www.heartfullovingpress.com

Please send me more information on:
__ Other books   ___ Speaking / Seminars   ___ Mailing Lists ___ Consulting

Name: _____
Address: _____
City: _____ State:_____ Zip: _____
Telephone: (___)_____ E-Mail Address: _____

Book Orders
Please send me the following books.
I understand that I may return any of them for a full refund if I am not satisfied.

How To Be The Best Lover – A Guide For Teenage Boys $19.95 x ___ = $_____
How To Be A Family – The Operating Manual $19.95 x ___ = $_____
First Love / Remembrances $19.95 x ___ = $_____

Sales tax: Please add 7.75% ($1.55 per book) for
orders shipped to California addresses. $_____

Shipping & Handling:
U.S. $4. for the first book and $2. for each additional book.
International: $9. for the first book and $5 for each additional book. $_____

Total: $_____

Payment (please circle one): CHECK / CREDIT CARD: VISA, MASTERCARD, AMEX

Card Number: _____ Exp. Date: ____ / ____
Name on card: _____
Signature: _____